SINGAPOREAN COOKING

by **MRS LEONG YEE SOO**

EASTERN UNIVERSITIES PRESS SDN. BHD.
SINGAPORE ■ KUALA LUMPUR ■ HONGKONG

EASTERN UNIVERSITIES PRESS SDN. BHD.
112 F, Block 5, Boon Keng Road, Singapore 12.
134, Jalan Kasah, Damansara Heights, Kuala Lumpur.

Printed by Kyodo-Shing Loong.
[Photographs by Mun & Wong Photographers.]

Foreword

Mrs. Leong Yee Soo belongs to the generation of Straits 'nonyas' to whom good cuisine is an article of faith and a personal challenge.

Having spent the major part of her adult life in thinking, talking, experimenting and teaching food preparation, Mrs. Leong feels that she can contribute nothing better to society than to pass on the results of her research and experience. She regrets that the fine art of cooking is fast dying out with women taking up jobs and with instant foods, frozen dinners, snack-bars and take-aways so much in evidence.

Realising the role of women in this nuclear age Mrs. Leong has planned her meals with a keen eye on the cost and quality of ingredients, time in preparation, calorie content, food value, etc. She has also summoned to her aid modern kitchen equipment and has so simplified her procedure that dabbling in the kitchen can be a source of fun.

The recipes will speak for themselves. There are house-hold staples that have fortified the oriental home for generations, meals for large and small groups, young and old, in and out of doors, tit-bits, snatched meals and feasts for special occasions.

I would recommend this book of tested recipes for every kitchen shelf, for not only is wholesome food conducive to health and happiness, but, like "mother's cooking", it will be affectionately remembered and will go a long way towards fostering goodwill and happy relationships.

Mrs. Goh Kok Kee.
J.P., M.B.E.

Author's acknowledgements

My sincere thanks go to Mrs. Rosa Lee, Mrs. Dorothy Norris, Miss Marie Choo, and Miss Patricia Lim who, by their co-operation and inspiring ideas, have made this book possible.

My thanks are due also to Mrs. Dinah Sharif, Miss Iris Kng, Miss Chau Mei Po, Mrs. Irene Oei, and Miss Monica Funk who gave up so much of their precious time in helping me type the recipes.

I would also like to thank all those who have been so helpful in the preparation and arrangement of the food and cakes for the photography sessions.

WEIGHTS AND MEASURES

American measuring spoons are used in this book. All measures are level except when stated. British measuring spoons are slightly bigger in capacity.

Mass

1 oz	–	30 g
4 oz	–	115 g
8 oz ($\frac{1}{2}$ lb)	–	225 g
16 oz (1 lb)	–	455 g
2 lb	–	905 g

Capacity

1 fl oz	–	30 ml
4 fl oz	–	115 ml
8 fl oz	–	225 ml
16 fl oz	–	455 ml

Temperature

°F	Gas Regulo	°C
225	1	105
250	2	120
275	3	135
300	4	150
325	5	165
350	6	175
375	7	190
400	8	205
425	9	220
450	10	230

Pre-heat oven 15 minutes before use.

CONTENTS

LIST OF ILLUSTRATIONS

EQUIPMENT FOR THE KITCHEN

Suggested list

(14) Biscuit cutters
    Bottle opener
    Bread bin
    Bread board and knife
(5) Cake spatula
    Cake tins
    Can opener
(24) Chinese frying slice
    Chopping boards
(29) Chopsticks
    Colanders
    Cooling racks
(18) Doughnut cutters
(12) Egg cutter (for wedges)
(13) Egg cutter (for slices)
    Enamel basins
    Electric blender
    Electric cake mixer
    Electric kettle
    Electric mincer
    Electric rice cooker
    Electric toaster
(4) Fish slice
(2) Frying slice
    Granite block with a granite rolling pin
(26) Grater
(28) Ice pick
(23) Icing bag
(16) Icing tube
    Jelly moulds
    Juicer
    Kitchen knives
(21) Kitchen scissors
    Kitchen timer
    Knife sharpener
(9) Lid for wok
    Ladles
(30) Ladles for making yam basket

    Mallet — meat tenderizer
    Measuring cups
(22) Measuring spoons
    Oven-proof dishes
(3) Palette knife
(20) Pastry brush
(17) Pastry pincers
(19) Pastry roller
(7) Pestle and mortar or pounder
    Pie tins
(11) Potato masher (ricer)
(10) Rack for steaming

(25) Roasting fork
    Rolling pin
    Saucepans
(15) Scraper
(1) Sieve
    Skewers
    Spiral egg whisk
    Steamer
(27) Tongs
(6) Wire mesh ladles
(8) Wok (kuali), cast iron
    Wok (kuali), aluminium

Uses of kitchen equipment

Aluminium frying pans:
Suitable for deep-frying as they retain a steady heat and give food a nice golden brown colour. Frying chillied paste in an aluminium pan will give the mixture a natural bright colour whereas an iron wok (kuali) will turn it darkish and may give it a slight taste of iron.

Aluminium saucepan:
The heavy flat-bottomed pan is the best buy. It is suitable for both the electric or gas stove. Food is cooked easily without burning. A thin saucepan will buckle when it is overheated and will not be in contact with the electric hot plate.

Enamel saucepan:
Enamel saucepans are more suitable for soups and certain types of food that contain acid like tamarind or vinegar. Chipped enamelware is vulnerable to rust.

Iron wok (kuali):
Most Chinese prefer the iron wok to the aluminium one chiefly because the iron wok can retain extreme heat before the other ingredients are added. Ingredients will cook in a shorter time, keep their taste, and retain their crispness. The most important point to remember is that fried food and pounded ingredients will not stick to the bottom of the wok when it is well heated.

To season an iron wok:
Boil some grated coconut and water till dry [the water should fill up to three-quarters of the wok]. Stir occa-sionally till the coconut turns black, approximately 3 — 4 hours.
Daily care: Do not use any detergent. Wipe wok well after each wash. If it is to be stored for a long period, grease wok lightly to prevent rust.

Stainless steel pans:
Stainless steel pans look attractive and are easily cleaned, but do not heat evenly. Food burns easily, too.

Copper pans:
Copper pans are rarely used for our Asian recipes. A copper pan has its own rare qualities. Salted mustard has a very bright green colour when boiled in a copper pan. It is very rarely used however as it is very expensive.

China clay pot:
Braising and stewing of chicken and pork are usually done in the China clay pot. It simmers food very nicely without burning and has a lower rate of evaporation than other saucepans. It also retains any special flavour of the food and is widely used in Chinese homes. It is also used to cook rice and porridge. Buy one with a smooth, glazed finish.

Pounder (pestle and mortar):
Insist on local granite which is white with black/grey spots. To season the pounder, grind a small handful of fine sea sand in the mortar until both the pestle and mortar are reasonably smooth.

GLOSSARY OF CULINARY TERMS

Baking   To cook in dry heat, usually in an oven.

Barbecue   To roast or broil whole such as a pig or fowl, usually on a revolving frame over coals. To cook slices of marinated meat over a coal fire.

Baste   To pour melted fat, dripping or sauce over roasting food in order to moisten.

Beat   A quick regular motion that lifts a mixture over and over to make it smooth and to introduce air.

Blanch
   (i) Whiten, i.e., cover with cold water, bring to the boil, strain and remove skins as for almonds.
  (ii) To pour boiling water over food then drain and rinse with cold water.

Blend   Mix to a smooth paste with a little cold or hot liquid.

Boil   To cook rapidly in liquid over very high heat till bubbles rise continually.

Bouillon   Clear seasoned soup made usually from lean beef or chicken.

Braise   To cook meat in fat, then simmer in a covered saucepan or dish with a small amount of water till tender.

Capon   A castrated male chicken.

Caramelize   To heat dry sugar or foods containing sugar till light brown.

Condiments   Food seasoning e.g. salt, pepper, light and dark soya sauces, mustard, vinegar, herbs and spices.

Croutons   Small squares of fried bread or toast.

Custard   A mixture mainly of eggs and milk which is steamed or baked. It may be sweetened for a dessert.

Dredge   To sprinkle with flour or sugar.

Fillets   Pieces of fish or undercuts of meat, free of skin and bone.

Fold in   To mix cake mixture by lifting a part of the batter from the bottom through the rest of the mixture over on to itself without releasing air bubbles.

Fritters   Meat, fish, fruit or vegetables [whole or chopped up] covered with batter and usually deep-fried in fat.

Frying
   (i) To cook in an open pan in a little hot fat.
  (ii) Deep-frying is cooking by immersion in smoking hot fat.

Garnish   To decorate savoury food with sprigs of parsley, sliced lemon wedges, cooked or uncooked vegetables, grated yolk of egg and cheese, croutons, pink sugar, etc.

Glaze   To brush over pastries, bread, etc. with a liquid such as eggs, milk or water and sugar to improve the appearance.

Grill   To cook by direct heat on a grill iron or under a red hot grill; used for small tender pieces of meat, fish, etc.

Knead   To mix by hand or electric dough hook. To press, fold and stretch. Usually

Marinate   applied to dough. To turn the outside edges of dough into the middle.
An oil and acid, or sauce in which food is allowed to stand to give flavour to meats, salads, etc.

Mince   To chop very fine. An electric mincer may be used.

Par-boil   To boil raw food until partially cooked as for carrots, cauliflower, cabbage, etc.

Poach   To cook gently in water below boiling point to which a little vinegar is added as for eggs. Salt and a little oil are usually added for fish.

Roast   To cook with a little fat in a hot oven. Fat from the baking tin is used to baste the meat or poultry, from time to time.

Roe   Eggs of fish.

Score   To cut very lightly or to mark with lines before cooking. Applied to roast pork, fish.

Simmer   To cook just below boiling point. Small bubbles rise occasionally to the surface of the liquid.

Stew   To cook slowly until tender in just sufficient liquid to cover the food. A stew may be cooked in a covered saucepan or casserole, on a hot plate or in the oven.

Steam   To cook seasoned food in a steamer over a pan of boiling water.

Stock   A rich extract from meat, fish, poultry, bones, etc., used as a basis for soups or gravies. Chicken or beef cubes can be substituted.

Tepid liquid   Two parts of cold liquid to one part boiling.

HELPFUL HINTS

To fry shallots:
Slice shallots thinly and dip in salt water for a while. Rinse and drain well. Scatter sliced shallots on to absorbent paper to dry or roll up in a tea towel for $\frac{1}{2}$ hour. Heat oil for deep-frying till smoking hot. Add the sliced shallots and stir-fry over high heat till shallots turn light brown. Reduce the heat, keep stirring all the time until the shallots are light golden brown. Remove at once with a wire sieve to drain the oil and scatter on to absorbent paper to cool. Keep in a clean, dry, bottle immediately. The shallots keep crisp for months in an airtight bottle.

To fry pounded garlic:
Pound garlic or use an electric mincer to mince the garlic. Place garlic in a wire sieve and immerse in salt water. Drain. Use a thin piece of muslin to squeeze out the water. Heat an iron wok (kuali). Heat oil for deep-frying till smoking hot. Place the garlic in, stir-fry till garlic turns light brown. Reduce the heat to very low and keep stirring till garlic is light golden brown. Remove at once with a wire sieve and scatter on to absorbent paper. Cool and store as for crispy shallots.

Note:
The crispy shallots and garlic do not retain so much oil when the heat is increased just before removing from wok.

To fry anchovies:
Place anchovies on a tray to dry under a warm grill till very dry. Remove any stone or grit before frying. Heat oil for deep-frying in an aluminium wok (kuali) till very hot. Add the anchovies, fry over moderate heat till crisp right through. Drain and scatter anchovies on to absorbent paper to cool. Keep in a dry airtight container.

To make croutons [crisp diced bread]:
Cut overnight bread into small cubes. Put in a warm grill for $\frac{1}{2}$ hour. Heat oil for deep-frying and add the diced bread. Fry over moderate heat till light golden brown. Drain and scatter on to absorbent paper to remove the oil. Cool before storing in an airtight container.

To roast groundnuts:
Rub groundnuts in a perforated plastic colander to remove small stones and grit. Pre-heat grill till very hot. Place groundnuts in grill pan under grill. Stir from time to time till light brown and crisp, about $\frac{1}{2}$ to $\frac{3}{4}$ hour. Reduce heat for the last 15 minutes of cooking time. Cool for a while. Rub groundnuts with hands whilst hot to remove the skin. Cool before keeping in an airtight container.

To cook spaghetti:
Simmer spaghetti in salted boiling water for 15 minutes. Drain, add some oil or a knob of butter whilst hot. Keep spaghetti warm by placing it in a covered bowl over a pan of simmering water.

To cook dried egg noodles:
Place one packet noodles in 1·4 litres (48 fl oz) boiling water with one chicken cube and 1 tablespoon oil.

Boil gently till noodles separate. Remove and immerse immediately in cold water. Drain immediately in a colander.

To cook rice:
Wash rice till water runs clear. Use 55 ml (2 fl oz) of water for each 30 g (1 oz) of rice. For 455 g (16 oz) of rice, use between 795 – 910 ml (28–32 fl oz) water, depending on the quality of the rice. Boil the rice till the water evaporates, leaving steam holes when dry. Reduce heat to low and cook for a further $\frac{1}{2}$ hour. 455 g (16 oz) of rice is sufficient for 8 servings.

To boil fresh bamboo:
Remove the furry covering from bamboo shoots. Cut into 2 or 3 pieces and boil for 2 hours. Cool before cutting.

To scald dried rice vermicelli:
Place rice vermicelli in a saucepan of boiling water for 2 minutes. Drain in a colander.

To mix dried spicy ingredients for fish curry:
Wash and dry the following thoroughly in the sun.
   Fennel seeds, fenugreek, skinned black beans, poppy seeds, cumin.
Mix 2 tablespoonfuls of each well and keep in a clean dry bottle. Store in refrigerator for future use.
(Available at Indian grocers as 'rempah tumis' for fish.)

Frying:
1. The pan should be very hot before you pour in the oil; but do not make the oil smoking hot. To get the best results when frying vegetables:-
   (a) Use an iron wok (kuali) as it can take and retain extreme heat, which is most important.
   (b) Add the oil to a smoking hot wok. This prevents food from sticking to the bottom. But overheated fat or oil turns bitter and loses its fine flavour.

2. (a) For deep-frying, the oil must be smoky, that is when a faint haze of smoke rises from the oil. It is then ready for frying.
   (b) When deep-frying in large quantities, put enough food in the pan and keep the oil boiling all the time.
   (c) Bring the fat back to smoking hot, each time you put in food to be fried.
   (d) When frying large pieces of meat or a whole chicken, the heat must be very high for the first 5 minutes to seal in the juices, then lower heat for the rest of the cooking time so as to give the meat or chicken a nice golden colour as well as to let it be cooked right through.

3. (a) After frying food that is coated with flour or breadcrumbs [this also seals in the meat juices], filter the oil through a wire sieve lined thinly with cotton wool. The oil will come clean of sediments.
   (b) Add more fresh oil to the strained oil for future use.

4. Oil that has been used to deep-fry fish and prawns

should be kept separately for future use, i.e., for cooking fish and prawns only.

5. You may clarify hot oil by squeezing some lemon juice on to it but remember to turn off the heat first. Strain and store for future use.

6. Butter will not take intense heat when frying; so put in some oil before the butter.

7. Dust food with seasoned flour before coating with or dipping in batter for frying.

Vegetables:

1. To fry leafy vegetables, the leafy part should be separated from the stalk. The stalks should be placed in the pan together with any ingredients to be cooked. Stir-fry for a minute or so before adding the leaves.

2. (a) For boiling and scalding vegetables, boil a saucepan of water over very high heat. When the water is boiling, add some salt, sugar and a tablespoonful of oil.

   (b) Add the stalks, cook for $\frac{1}{2}$ minute and then add the leaves. Cook for another $\frac{1}{2}$ minute. Use a wire ladle to lift the vegetables and drain in a colander.

   (c) Rinse under a running tap and drain well before use.

   (d) Vegetables like long beans and cabbages should be cooked for 5—7 minutes only, to retain their sweetness and crispness.

   (e) When boiling bean sprouts it is important to place them in boiling water for 1 minute. Do not add any oil. Lift and drain in a wire ladle. Transfer to a basin of cold water and soak for 10 minutes or till cold. Spread thinly in a colander, till ready for use. The bean sprouts will then keep without 'souring'.

Pork chops:

Pork chops should be cooked in immediate heat in a very hot pan or grilled under a hot grill. This will seal in the meat juices. Brown on both sides, turning over twice; lower to medium heat till done, about 15—20 minutes.

Bacon:

Cut off the rind and snip the fat in two or three places to prevent the bacon from curling when being fried.

Beef:

Fillet steak is the best and most tender of meat cuts; next comes sirloin, scotch porterhouse, rump and minute steak. Marinating a steak before cooking not only gives it a better flavour but also helps to make it tender. Minute steak, however, is best grilled or fried without marinating.

To prove yeast dough before shaping and baking:

Method 1:

Pre-heat oven to 105°C (225°F) or Regulo 1. Turn heat off. Place dough in lightly greased bowl, cover with damp cloth and place it in the oven. Leave oven door slightly open. Check dough after 10—15 minutes to see if it has doubled in bulk.

Method 2:

Fill three-quarters of a large saucepan or basin with hot water, place a wine rack over the saucepan or basin and place the dough in a bowl on the rack. Cover with a large damp cloth and allow dough to rise till double in bulk in 20–30 minutes.

Method 3:

Place dough in a warmed, lightly greased bowl. Cover with a damp cloth, leave in a warm place and allow to rise till double in bulk in 40 minutes to 1 hour.

Selecting meat, poultry and seafood

Pork:

Pork should be pink, the fat very white and the skin thin.

Beef:

Choose meat that is light red and the cross-grain smooth and fine. The same applies to mutton. Do not buy dark coloured meat with fat that is yellow.

Chicken:

Fresh local chickens have a much better taste and flavour than frozen ones. Frozen chicken is more suitable for roasting, frying or grilling. Fresh local chicken is usually boiled, steamed or fried with vegetables. When buying a local chicken, select one with a white, smooth skin. The tip of the breastbone should be soft and pliable when pressed with the thumb.

Duck:

Select as for chicken. The smaller ones are mostly used for soups and the larger ducks for roasting or braising.

Fish:

When buying fish, first of all make sure that the flesh is firm to the touch. The eyes should be shiny, the gills blood-red and the scales silvery white. Squeezing lemon juice over fish will whiten it and keep it firm when boiling or steaming.

Mix tamarind, salt and some sugar to marinate fish pieces for $\frac{1}{2}$ hour before cooking curries or tamarind dishes.

Prawns:

Fresh prawns are firm to the touch, with their shells shiny. The head is attached fast to the body. Avoid buying prawns that smell bad and with their heads almost falling off.

Cuttlefish:

When cuttlefish is very fresh, the body is well-rounded, firm and shiny. The head is stuck fast to the body and the inky pouch in the stomach is firmly attached.

IMPORTANT POINTS TO NOTE

Coconut: Coconut referred to in all recipes is fresh coconut unless specified. Coconut is used mainly for its rich milky juice so necessary for Asian dishes like curries, sambals and cakes.

Grated white coconut is coconut that is grated after the brown skin has been removed. This form is required for certain cakes like *Kueh Ko Swee*.

Use a piece of muslin to squeeze small handfuls of grated coconut so as to get more milk. No 1 milk is got by squeezing the grated coconut without adding water. When water is added to the grated coconut after the first squeeze, the milky liquid extracted is called the No 2 milk.

Garlic: A bulb of garlic consists of several small cloves.

Spices: It is advisable to buy the different types of spices in whole pieces rather than in powder form. Wash, dry and grind them finely. Put in airtight containers or bottles and keep in the refrigerator for future use.

Lemon grass: Lemon grass gives a pleasant fragrance to cooked dishes. Use lemon rind as a substitute only when this is not available. The fragrance comes from the end of the stalk, about 7 cm (3 in) from the root end.

The green outer layer is usually taken off before use. To "bruise" lemon grass, bash with the flat surface of a cleaver or chopper.

Candlenuts: If unavailable, use almonds, cashew nuts, Brazil nuts or macadamia nuts. Their nutty flavour is the nearest to the candlenut.

Turmeric: Fresh turmeric is usually used for 'nonya' dishes because of its flavour and colour. Oriental dishes, especially curries, need dry turmeric or turmeric powder.

Lard: The oil extracted from pork fat after it has been fried is called lard. Dice the pork fat before frying. Do not overburn the cubes otherwise the oil extracted will be dark and bitter. Unlike butter or margarine, lard can take intense heat without burning so it is most suitable for food that has to be cooked over high heat.

Butter: Butter begins to burn and turns black as soon as it gets into a heated pan. When a recipe calls for ingredients to be fried in butter, heat a little oil in the pan before adding the butter.

Screw pine leaves: These give a special fragrance. There is no substitute. Before tying into a knot, tear lengthwise to get the strongest fragrance.

NONYA CAKES

1 Kueh Sarlat

(Glutinous rice cake with custard topping)

COCONUT MILK:

1·6 kg (3½ lb) grated coconut, white
1½ teaspoons salt
1 tablespoon castor sugar

1. Using a piece of muslin, squeeze grated coconut to obtain approximately 625 ml (22 fl oz) No 1 milk. Set aside 455 ml (16 fl oz) for the custard topping.
2. Pour the remaining 170 ml (6 fl oz) No 1 milk into a separate jug for the glutinous rice. Add the salt and castor sugar and stir till dissolved. Set aside. Add 340 ml (12 fl oz) water to grated coconut and squeeze for No 2 milk. Measure 225 ml (8 fl oz) and set aside.

CUSTARD TOPPING:

1 tablespoon flour
1 tablespoon cornflour
10 screw pine leaves, pounded to a
fine pulp
370 g (13 oz) coarse sugar
10 eggs, beaten lightly
1 teaspoon green food colouring

1. Mix 4 tablespoonfuls from 455 ml of the No 1 milk with the two types of flour till smooth.
2. Add the rest of the milk to the pounded screw pine leaves. Mix well and squeeze with a fine muslin.
3. Blend the milk with the flour mixture. Set aside.
4. Cook the sugar and beaten eggs in a heavy-bottomed aluminium saucepan over a very low heat. Stir constantly till sugar dissolves.
5. Remove from the heat. Add the flour mixture and green food colouring. Stir well and set aside.

GLUTINOUS RICE:

625 g (22 oz) glutinous rice, washed
and soaked overnight
6 screw pine leaves, tied into a
knot

1. Drain and steam glutinous rice with screw pine leaves over rapidly boiling water for 15 minutes. Make steam holes in glutinous rice with handle of wooden spoon before steaming.
2. Remove glutinous rice to a saucepan, pour in the No 2 milk. Mix well and cover for 5 minutes.
3. Return glutinous rice to the steamer. Steam for another 7 minutes. Remove to saucepan and mix well with the salted No 1 milk. Cover for another 5 minutes.
4. Steam glutinous rice again for 5 minutes.
5. Remove glutinous rice to a round tray, 30 cm (12 in) in diameter and 5 cm (2 in) deep. Press down firmly with a banana leaf or a thick piece of soft plastic.

To steam kueh sarlat:

1. Steam tray of glutinous rice over boiling water for 15 minutes.
2. Re-heat the egg mixture for 2 minutes, stirring all the time. Pour it over the glutinous rice. Cover and steam over a moderately high heat for 15 minutes or till mixture changes colour and sets, forming slight ridges on the surface.
3. Reduce heat to very low and continue steaming for 1 hour, or till a knife comes out clean when inserted into the centre of top green layer. Remove and place tray on a wire rack to cool completely before cutting cake.

Note:
Make steam holes each time using a chopstick when re-steaming glutinous rice. From time to time, wipe water collected on the underside of lid of iron wok. Any droplet will cause discolouration of the cake. Add boiling water to iron wok when necessary.

2 Kueh Dadar

(Coconut rolls with coconut sauce)

BATTER:

A
- 565 g (20 oz) grated coconut, white, for No 1 milk
- 455 ml (16 fl oz) water
- $\frac{1}{2}$ teaspoon salt
- 2 tablespoons oil
- 4 large eggs, lightly beaten
- 225 g (8 oz) flour
- 1 tablespoon sago flour
- Different shades of food colouring

1. Extract 225 ml (8 fl oz) No 1 milk from grated coconut. Set aside. Add 455 ml water to grated coconut and squeeze again to obtain 225 ml (8 fl oz) No 2 milk. Set aside.
2. Mix the two types of coconut milk together with A in a bowl till smooth. Strain into another bowl. Divide batter into three or four portions. Add a few drops of different shades of food colouring to each portion. Stir well. Let stand for $\frac{1}{2}$ hour.
3. Heat an omelette pan till hot. Remove pan from the heat and grease base. Pour just enough batter to cover the base of the pan thinly. Fry pancake till edge curls slightly upwards and pancake is able to slip easily away from pan. Pile pancakes on a plate. Cool before filling.
4. Fill each pancake with 2 tablespoonfuls of coconut filling. Fold to enclose filling, then roll.

FILLING:

A
- 3 tablespoons sugar
- 285 g (10 oz) grated palm sugar
- 3 tablespoons water
- 6 screw pine leaves
- 565 g (20 oz) grated coconut, white
- 1 tablespoon sago flour mixed with 2 tablespoons water

1. Boil A in an iron wok (kuali) until the sugar turns syrupy.
2. Add grated coconut and lower the heat. Stir mixture constantly till almost dry.
3. Add the sago flour mixture. Stir thoroughly. Cook for another 5 minutes. Remove to a tray to cool.

SAUCE:

- 680 g (24 oz) grated coconut, white
- 455 ml (16 fl oz) water
- 3 tablespoons plain flour
- 55 g (2 oz) wet rice flour or 3 tablespoons rice-flour
- 1 teaspoon salt
- 1 tablespoon sugar
- 6 screw pine leaves, tied into a knot

1. Squeeze grated coconut for No 1 milk. Set aside. Add 455 ml water to grated coconut and squeeze again for No 2 milk. Measure milk and add water to bring it up to 855 ml (30 fl oz).
2. Mix 225 ml (8 fl oz) of the No 2 milk with the two types of flour. Set aside.
3. Bring the rest of the No 2 milk together with the salt, sugar and screw pine leaves to nearly boiling point in a saucepan.
4. Remove saucepan from the heat. Add the flour mixture gradually to the hot milk, stirring all the time. Add No 1 milk.

5. Return saucepan to the heat and allow mixture to boil over a very low heat, stirring constantly. Remove and pour sauce into a large bowl to cool.
6. Serve with grated coconut rolls.

Wet Rice or Glutinous Rice Flour

To 22 oz of fine rice or glutinous rice flour, gradually add 15 – 17 oz of cold water and stir till it becomes a firm paste. Use the amount required for each recipe and keep the remainder in the freezer for future use. The paste will keep in the freezer for 1 – 2 months if kept in plastic bags flattened to one inch thick slabs.

Recommended brands: "Superior Quality Thai Rice and Glutinous Rice Flour" (Three Elephant Heads trade mark); "Fine Rice Flour" (Sea Gull trade mark); freshly ground wet rice or glutinous rice flour obtainable from Singapore markets, e.g. Joo Chiat Market.

Note:
For the pancakes, use an omelette pan with a 16.5 cm (6½ in) base.

[22 pieces]

Kueh Dadar (2), Kueh Bengka Pulot (5), Kueh Sarlat (1).

3 Kueh Bongkong

(Rice savouries)

Satay sticks
225 g (8 oz) palm sugar
2 tablespoons sugar
855 ml (30 fl oz) water
565 g (20 oz) grated coconut, white

A {
285 g (10 oz) wet rice flour*
1 tablespoon non-glutinous plain flour
$\frac{1}{2}$ tablespoon green pea flour, 'Flower' brand
$1\frac{1}{4}$ teaspoons salt
1 tablespoon sugar
}

4 screw pine leaves, tied into a knot
25 pieces of banana leaves, 20 cm × 23 cm (8 in × 9 in) — washed, scalded and drained in a colander
25 pieces of screw pine leaves, each 4 cm ($1\frac{1}{2}$ in) in length
25 pieces of banana leaves, 23 cm × 5 cm (9 in × 2 in) — washed and wiped dry

1. Cut the satay sticks slantwise into 6 cm ($2\frac{1}{2}$ in) lengths to sharpen both ends.
2. Grate the palm sugar into a bowl. Add the other type of sugar and mix well. Set aside.
3. Add 855 ml water to the grated coconut and squeeze hard in small handfuls, using a piece of muslin, to obtain 1·4 litres (48 fl oz) milk. Add more water if necessary. Set 170 ml (6 fl oz) aside for steaming with the cakes.
4. Combine A in a basin. Add 425 ml (15 fl oz) of the milk and blend by hand. Set aside.
5. In a saucepan, heat the rest of the milk and the knotted screw pine leaves. Remove saucepan from the heat and pour the milk gradually into the flour mixture. Stir till well blended.
6. Return the milk and flour mixture to the saucepan. Cook over a low heat, stirring all the time till the mixture thickens and turns pasty. Remove saucepan from the heat and set aside.

Wrapping and steaming (See next page)

1. Place the bigger piece of banana leaf in a shallow bowl.
2. Heap two tablespoonfuls of the cooked paste on to the centre of the leaf.
3. Place a tablespoonful of the mixed sugar on the paste.
4. Sandwich the sugar with another tablespoonful of paste.
5. Finally, add a piece of screw pine leaf and a tablespoonful of coconut milk. Fold as shown in the photograph. Use the smaller piece of banana leaf to wrap the folded bundle before fastening it with a satay stick.
6. Repeat the process till all the paste is used up. Steam the bundles over rapidly boiling water for 10 – 15 minutes.

[Makes 20 bundles]

*See "Wet Rice Flour" on page 21.

To fold Kueh Bongkong:

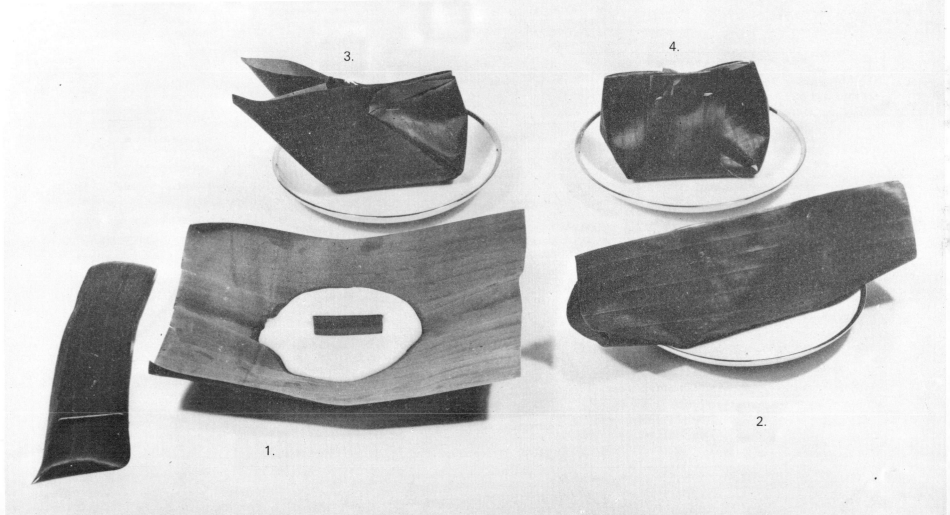

4 *Kueh Khoo Moh Ho*

(Bean buns)

BUNS: (using an electric mixer)

340 g (12 oz) sweet potatoes, skinned
    and cut into pieces
    Water
200 g (7 oz) sugar
    $\frac{1}{2}$ teaspoon salt
140 ml (5 fl oz) oil
565 g (20 oz) plain flour
225 g (8 oz) self-raising flour
340 g (12 oz) bread dough
 40 pieces of 4 cm (1$\frac{1}{2}$ in) square
    greaseproof paper

1. Boil the sweet potatoes in 680 ml
    (24 fl oz) water till cooked. Remove
    the sweet potatoes and pass them
    through a potato ricer whilst hot.
    Set aside.
2. Dissolve the sugar and salt in 455 ml
    (16 fl oz) of the hot sweet potato
    stock. Stir in the oil and set aside.
    Keep warm.
3. Sift the flour together. Place sifted
    flour, mashed sweet potatoes and
    bread dough [broken into small
    pieces] in a mixing bowl. Fix dough
    hook to electric mixer.
4. Add half of the warm sweet potato

stock [Step 2]. Switch mixer to
No 1 or low, and beat mixture till it
becomes gluey. Add the rest of the
sweet potato stock and continue
mixing till dough turns glossy and
comes clean off sides of bowl—about
15 minutes.

5. Remove dough to a lightly greased
    bowl. Cover with a damp cloth and
    allow dough to rise to double its bulk.
6. Place dough on a well-floured board
    and knead lightly with a little flour.
7. Divide dough into four parts. Roll
    each part like a sausage. Cut the
    rolls into 10—12 equal portions. Roll
    each portion lightly into a ball.
8. Flatten each ball slightly to hold a
    ball of sweet filling. Bring up the
    edges of the dough to cover the
    filling.
9. Seal the edges and form dough into a
    neat round bun. Place a piece of
    greaseproof paper on the sealed end.
    Place buns apart on steamer trays and
    leave to rise in a warm place for
    $\frac{1}{2}$ hour.

FILLING:

565 g (20 oz) skinned green beans;
    washed, soaked overnight, and
    drained
140 ml (5 fl oz) water
  8 screw pine leaves, tied into a
    knot
625 g (22 oz) coarse sugar

1. Steam the green beans till soft, about
    20 minutes, and pass them through
    the ricer whilst hot. Set aside.
2. Boil the water in an iron wok (kuali).
    Add the screw pine leaves and sugar
    and boil over a low heat till the sugar
    turns syrupy.
3. Add the mashed beans, mix well and
    cook mixture until almost dry, stirring
    all the time. Remove the screw pine
    leaves and let the mixture cool.
4. Form the sweet filling into equal
    rounds [each the size of a walnut]
    and place them on a tray. Flatten
    each ball of filling slightly before
    placing it on the dough.

To steam buns:

Place the buns in a steamer to steam over rapidly boiling water for 10 minutes. Do not remove lid of steamer till buns are cooked. Serve hot.

Note:
1. *You can prepare the filling 1–2 days ahead. Keep in a plastic container and put in a refrigerator.*
2. *Wipe water from under the lid of steamer each time before steaming each tray.*
3. *Do not lift lid of steamer until buns are cooked.*
4. *Let buns cool on a cake rack after steaming. This will prevent the buns from becoming soggy at the bottom.*
5. *Cooled buns can be kept in the refrigerator and re-steamed. Cover the buns with a piece of kitchen paper when storing in a container.*
6. *When not using an electric mixer, knead dough on a floured board till smooth and satiny.*

Rich Fruit Cake (28), Kueh Lapis Beras (6), Speckok Kueh Lapis Batavia (5), Kueh Khoo Moh Ho (4).

5 *Speckok Kueh Lapis Batavia*

(Indonesian layer cake)

455 g (16 oz) butter
1 teaspoon mixed spice*
115 g (4 oz) flour
17 egg yolks
5 egg whites
255 g (9 oz) sugar
2 tablespoons brandy

1. Beat butter till creamy.
2. Sift mixed spice and flour together.
3. Place egg yolks and egg whites in two separate bowls.
4. Beat egg yolks with 200 g (7 oz) sugar till thick.
5. Beat egg whites with the remaining sugar till thick.
6. Fold in alternately, the egg yolk mixture and the egg white mixture to the creamed butter, adding a little flour each time. Lastly, add the brandy.

To bake the cake:
1. Grease bottom and sides of tin with butter.
2. Cut a piece of greaseproof paper to fit base of tin exactly. Place paper in tin and grease with butter.
3. Heat grill moderately hot. Place greased tin under grill for a minute. Remove and place in one ladleful of cake mixture. Spread mixture evenly and bake for 5 minutes or till light brown. Remove tin from grill and, using a fine sharp skewer or satay stick, prick top of cake to prevent air bubbles from forming.
4. Add another ladleful of cake mixture. Bake and repeat process as for the first layer, till the cake mixture is used up. Remove cake from tin at once. Turn it over, top side up, on to a cooling rack to cool for $\frac{1}{2}$ hour.

*See "Mixed Spice" on page 35.

6 *Kueh Lapis Beras*

(Rainbow layer cake)

570 ml (20 fl oz) water, to be added to the coconut
680 g (24 oz) grated coconut, white
340 g (12 oz) wet rice flour*
225 g (8 oz) sago flour
$\frac{1}{4}$ teaspoon salt
455 g (16 oz) coarse sugar
285 ml (10 fl oz) water, to be boiled with the sugar
8 screw pine leaves, tied into a knot
Drops of different shades of food colouring

1. Add the 570 ml water to the grated coconut. Take small handfuls of it and squeeze for milk, using a piece of muslin.
2. Measure the milk and add water to bring it to 855 ml (30 fl oz).
3. Place the two types of flour and salt in a bowl; add the coconut milk a little at a time and mix till smooth. Set aside.
4. Boil the sugar, the 285 ml water and the screw pine leaves for 10 minutes over a moderate heat. Strain the syrup into a bowl. Measure it and add hot water if necessary to bring it to 425 ml (15 fl oz).

7 *Kueh Bangket*

(Tapioca crumble)

5. Pour the hot boiled syrup gradually into the flour mixture, stirring all the time till it is well blended.

6. Divide the flour mixture into four portions. Set aside one portion to remain uncoloured and add a few drops of different shades of food colouring to the other three portions. [Set aside 140 ml (5 fl oz) of the uncoloured mixture to be coloured dark red for the top layer.]

7. Grease an 18 cm (7 in) diameter × 5 cm (2 in) deep cake tin with oil. Place tin in steamer of rapidly boiling water. Pour 140 ml (5 fl oz) of a different coloured batter into the tin for each layer and steam for 5 – 6 minutes each time, till mixture is used up.

8. For the final top layer, use the dark red batter. Remove cake to cool for at least 7 – 8 hours before cutting.

Note:
Wipe the underlid of steamer from time to time. It is best to leave the cake overnight before cutting.

See "Wet Rice Flour" on page 21.

---

455 g (16 oz) rice flour
455 g (16 oz) tapioca flour

To prepare the flour

1. Stir rice flour and tapioca flour separately in a dry iron wok (kuali) over a low heat till very light and fluffy.

2. Keep overnight. Mix and sift the two types of flour together into a basin.

455 g (16 oz) grated coconut, white, for No 1 milk
5 eggs
395 g (14 oz) sugar
$\frac{3}{4}$ teaspoon salt

1. Using a piece of muslin, squeeze coconut for No 1 milk. Set aside.

2. Beat eggs and sugar till thick and creamy. Add the salt and No 1 milk. Beat till well blended.

3. Set aside 115 g (4 oz) of the sifted flour for dusting and 1 teacup of the egg mixture.

4. Mix the remaining egg mixture into the flour to form a dough. Take a handful of the dough and place it on a dusted board or a marble table top.

[Keep the rest of the dough covered with a damp cloth.]

5. Flatten the dough with the palm of your hand. Dust with flour and roll dough out to 0·5 cm ($\frac{1}{4}$ in) thickness.

6. Cut dough with a round pastry cutter. Pinch biscuit, using a jagged-edged pair of pincers [usually used for pineapple tarts], to form a pattern.

7. Mix leftover dough cuttings with another lot of new dough and a little of the beaten egg mixture each time. Mix to a smooth texture before rolling out and repeat process.

8. Place biscuits on greased trays and bake in a moderate oven at 175°C (350°F) or Regulo 6 for 20 – 30 minutes. Cool biscuits on a rack before storing in an airtight tin.

Note:
Roasted sesame seeds can be placed on the biscuits. Roll dough out to 0·5 cm ($\frac{1}{4}$ in) thickness. Brush with beaten egg white. Sprinkle toasted sesame seeds all over, pressing lightly with palm of hand. Use cutter to cut. Do not use pincers. Bake.

8 *Kueh Bengka Pulot*

(Glutinous rice cake)

A 20 cm (8 in) square banana leaf, for lining cake tin
680 g (24 oz) grated coconut, white, for No 1 milk
395 g (14 oz) coarse sugar
4 screw pine leaves tied into a knot
510 g (18 oz) wet glutinous rice flour*
115 g (4 oz) wet rice flour
$\frac{1}{2}$ teaspoon salt
340 g (12 oz) coarsely grated coconut, white

1. Grease the sides and base of a square cake tin, and line it with the banana leaf.
2. Extract 285 ml (10 fl oz) No 1 milk from the grated coconut. Set aside.
3. Cook the sugar, No 1 milk and the screw pine leaves in a heavy-bottomed aluminium saucepan over a low heat. Keep stirring all the time till the sugar dissolves. Remove from the heat.
4. Place the two types of wet flour in a basin.
5. Add the sugary mixture gradually to the flour. Mix till well blended. Return the mixture to the saucepan, and cook over a very low heat, stirring all the time, till the mixture becomes thick and gluey [half-cooked]. Remove from the heat, stir in salt and the coarsely grated coconut.
6. Pour mixture into cake tin and bake in oven at 190°C (375°F) or Regulo 7 for 15 minutes. Reduce heat to 175°C (350°F) or Regulo 6 and bake for 1 – 1½ hours or till cake is cooked. Leave cake in tin for 20 minutes before turning it on to a cake rack to cool before cutting.

*See "Wet Rice Flour" on page 21.

9 *Kueh Bolu Kukus*

(Steamed sponge cake)

A {
455 g (16 oz) flour
115 g (4 oz) self-raising flour
}
10 eggs
680 g (24 oz) castor sugar
1 big bottle ice cream soda or toddy, if available

1. Sift A together twice.
2. Prepare and line patty tins [specially made for steamed sponge cake] with cellophane or 'glass' paper. Boil water in steamer.
3. Beat eggs and sugar till very thick and creamy.
4. Fold in the flour and ice cream soda a little at a time.
5. Fill each patty tin to the rim with cake batter. Place tins in a steamer of rapidly boiling water. Cover and steam for 7–10 minutes. Do not lift the lid until cakes are cooked, [at least 7 minutes].
6. Remove cakes on to a wire rack to cool.

Note:
After the first 7 minutes of steaming, lift lid to see if cake is puffed and split slightly at top. Cake should be spongy and dry. Add some melted cocoa to make chocolate rice sponge cakes. Stir in a few drops of red food colouring for pink sponge cakes.

10 *Kueh Talam Ko Swee*

(Rice cake with coconut creme topping)

COCONUT CREME TOPPING:

570 g (20 oz) grated coconut, white
425 ml (15 fl oz) water
3 rounded tablespoons sago flour
3 rounded tablespoons plain flour
3 tablespoons green pea flour, 'Flower' brand
4 tablespoons rice flour
1 tablespoon sugar
1 teaspoon salt

1. Extract 225 ml (8 fl oz) No 1 coconut milk from grated coconut. Set aside in a bowl.
2. Add the 425 ml water to the grated coconut and squeeze again to obtain 400 ml (14 fl oz) No 2 milk. Set aside in a jug.
3. Combine the four types of flour in a bowl. Add 170 ml (6 fl oz) of the No 2 milk to blend with the flour.
4. Bring the remainder of the milk to nearly boiling point in a saucepan. Remove and gradually pour 170 ml (6 fl oz) of the hot milk into the flour mixture, stirring till smooth. Add the rest of the milk and keep stirring till mixture is well blended.
5. Return mixture to the saucepan, stir and cook over a low heat till nearly boiling.
6. Add the No 1 milk, sugar and salt and keep stirring till mixture begins to thicken and boil.
7. Remove from the heat. Set aside until ready to add to the steamed bottom layer.

RICE AND SAGO FLOUR LAYER:

140 g (5 oz) wet rice flour*
140 g (5 oz) sago flour
510 ml (18 fl oz) water
$1\frac{1}{2}$ tablespoons alkaline water**
225 g (8 oz) palm sugar
115 g (4 oz) sugar
6 screw pine leaves, tied into a knot

1. Place the two types of flour in a small basin. Add 230 ml (8 fl oz) of the water and the alkaline water. Mix till well blended. Set aside.
2. In a saucepan, boil the palm sugar, sugar, screw pine leaves and the remaining water for 5—10 minutes till the sugar dissolves.
3. Pour half of the boiled syrup through a sieve into the flour mixture. [Note: Stir flour mixture before adding syrup to prevent formation of lumps.] Add the rest of the syrup, stirring all the time, till well blended.
4. Pour mixture into a round tray, 23 cm (9 in) in diameter and 5 cm (2 in) deep. Steam in steamer of rapidly boiling water for 15 minutes.
5. Remove lid of steamer and wipe water from the underlid. Pour the boiled coconut creme over the steamed cake and continue steaming for another 7—10 minutes or until coconut creme is set.
6. Remove tray to rest on a cake rack to cool. Allow to cool for at least 4 hours before cutting cake.

Note:
Small bowls can be used to steam the cake. Fill $\frac{3}{4}$ of the bowls with the rice and sago flour mixture and steam for 6 minutes. Then add the coconut creme to fill the bowls. Steam for another 4—5 minutes. Remove from bowls when completely cooled.

*See "Wet Rice Flour" on page 21.
**See page 30.*

11 *Kueh Ko Swee*

(Rice cup cakes)

A {
285 g (10 oz) wet rice flour*
285 g (10 oz) sago flour
570 ml (20 fl oz) cold water
3 tablespoons alkaline water
}

B {
455 g (16 oz) palm sugar
225 g (8 oz) coarse sugar
10 screw pine leaves, cut into 5 cm (2 in) lengths
455 ml (16 fl oz) water
}

455 g (16 oz) grated coconut, white, mixed with a pinch of fine salt

1. Mix *A* in a bowl.
2. Boil *B* for 10 minutes.
3. Strain the hot boiled syrup gradually into the flour mixture, stirring with a wooden spoon till well mixed.
4. Steam small empty cups for 5 minutes. Fill cups with flour mixture and steam over a high heat for 7 minutes. Cool and remove cake from each cup. Roll cakes in grated coconut before serving.

To make alkaline water:
625 g (22 oz) white alkaline crystal balls, obtainable from local markets
680 ml (24 fl oz) hot water

1. Place alkaline crystal balls in a porcelain jar. Add the hot water and stir with a wooden spoon till the crystal balls dissolve. Allow to stand overnight.
2. Strain alkaline water through fine muslin. Store the alkaline water in a bottle for future use.

Note:
Prepared alkaline water can be kept for almost a year. Store in a bottle.

*See "Wet Rice Flour" on page 21.

Kueh Ko Swee

12 Jemput-jemput Pisang

(Banana fritters)

200 g (7 oz) grated coconut, white, for No 1 milk
4 eggs
225 g (8 oz) sugar
½ teaspoon salt
340 g (12 oz) self-raising flour
115 g (4 oz) grated coconut, white
10 – 12 bananas (pisang rajah), mashed
Oil for deep-frying

1. Using a piece of muslin, squeeze the coconut for No 1 milk.
2. In a large bowl, beat eggs and sugar to a thick cream. Add salt.
3. Stir the flour in gradually. Add the white grated coconut, mashed bananas and No 1 milk. Mix very lightly.
4. Heat oil for deep-frying till hot.
5. Drop a few spoonfuls of the batter into the hot oil and fry till light brown. Repeat process till batter is used up.
6. Remove fritters to absorbent paper to cool.

Note:
Turn fritters once over only when one side is brown. Do not pile the fritters when they are still hot.

13 Seray-kaya

(Rich egg custard)

905 g (32 oz) grated coconut, white
10 eggs, 565 g (20 oz) in weight
565 g (20 oz) coarse sugar
2 screw pine leaves, tied into a knot

1. Using a piece of muslin, squeeze grated coconut to obtain 400 ml (14 fl oz) No 1 milk.
2. Beat eggs and sugar till well mixed.
3. Heat egg mixture and screw pine leaves in an enamel container over a very low heat to dissolve the sugar — about 10 minutes. Keep stirring all the time with a wooden spoon. Remove from the heat. Take away the screw pine leaves.
4. Add the No 1 milk to the egg mixture. Strain into an enamel container.
5. Stand container of egg mixture on a rack in a saucepan of rapidly boiling water. Keep stirring with a wooden spoon until the egg mixture turns thick like custard cream, about ¾ hour.

To steam seray-kaya:
1. Wrap lid of container with a dry tea-towel. Place container, with lid on, on rack in a saucepan.
2. Add hot water to saucepan to measure 2·5 cm (1 in) from base of container. Cover saucepan and steam for 3 hours over a moderate heat. Do not stir.
3. Dry the underlid of the cover of the saucepan from time to time to prevent discolouration of the seray-kaya. Change tea-towel if necessary.

Note:
Take small handfuls of grated coconut when squeezing for No 1 milk. Add hot water to the saucepan when necessary. Seray-kaya is best steamed over a charcoal burner.

14 Kueh Bengka Ubi Kayu

(Tapioca cake)

A {
- 455 g (16 oz) sugar
- 4 eggs
- 1·8 kg (4 lb) skinned, grated tapioca
- 455 g (16 oz) grated coconut, white
- 85 g (3 oz) melted butter
- 1 teaspoon vanilla essence
- 455 g (16 oz) grated coconut, white, extract No 1 milk
- 55 g (2 oz) flour, sifted with 2 teaspoons baking powder
- $\frac{1}{2}$ teaspoon salt

1. Beat *A* till thick.
2. Mix grated tapioca, grated coconut, butter and vanilla essence with beaten egg mixture and coconut milk.
3. Add flour and salt. Mix well.
4. Place in a greased tin and bake in hot oven at 205°C (400°F) or Regulo 8 for $\frac{1}{2}$ hour. Reduce heat to 175°C (350°F) or Regulo 6. Continue baking for another one hour or till cake is done. Remove cake from oven and let cool completely before cutting.

15 Kueh Pisang

(Banana cake)

- 625 g (22 oz) grated coconut, white, for milk
- 455 ml (16 fl oz) water
- 6–8 bananas (pisang rajah)
- 1 packet green pea flour
- $\frac{3}{4}$ teaspoon salt
- 310 g (11 oz) sugar

1. Squeeze grated coconut for No 1 milk. Add 455 ml water to grated coconut and squeeze again. Mix the milk together and add water so that it measures 1·3 litres (44 fl oz).
2. Steam bananas with skin on till cooked, about 10–12 minutes. Cool, remove skin and slice bananas (1 cm thick).
3. Place the green pea flour in a heavy-bottomed aluminium saucepan. Add 1 teacup of the measured coconut milk and salt. Stir to blend. Set aside.
4. Cook the sugar and the rest of the coconut milk over a low heat, stirring constantly till nearly boiling. Remove.
5. Stir flour mixture in the saucepan, pour in the hot coconut milk gradually, stirring all the while. Cook it gently over a very low heat till it boils. Let it boil for $\frac{1}{2}$ minute, stirring all the time. Remove from the heat.
6. Add the sliced bananas and mix well.
7. Rinse a square 23 cm (9 in) × 5 cm deep tin. Pour in the mixture to set. Chill in refrigerator.

Note:
Banana leaves can also be used to wrap the banana cakes. Cut banana leaves into 18 cm × 18 cm (7 in × 7 in) pieces. Wash and scald leaves. Drain. Put 2–3 tablespoonfuls of the cooked mixture with a few slices of banana in the centre of each leaf. Wrap to form a neat rectangle 6 cm × 8 cm (2$\frac{1}{2}$ in × 3$\frac{1}{2}$ in). Pile wrapped banana cakes in a square tray to chill in refrigerator.

Kueh Bengka Ubi Kayu (14),
Pulot Seray-kaya (13)

Kueh Pisang (15)

33

WESTERN CAKES

Hints for Cakes

Baking Powder — One brand is as good as another. Sift flour and baking powder two to three times before adding it to the creamed mixture.

Biscuits — The dough should be left in the refrigerator to cool before it is rolled and cut. It will hold its shape and be easier to handle.

Black Treacle — Only certain cakes need black treacle. If it is not available, a dark caramel may be used.

Bread-making — Thorough kneading by hand or using an electric dough hook to beat the dough till smooth will give a good rise and a fine texture. When dough leaves the hand clean, it is ready to be covered and left in a warm place to prove till double its size. On cold days the dough can be placed under a warm grill or in a very slow oven with the door open. Keep watch to see that the dough has not over-risen.

Butter — Use the best quality butter.

Caramel — This is made from heating sugar and water till thick and golden in colour. As soon as the sugar turns slightly brown at the sides of the pan, remove it from the heat and allow it to darken. Bring back to the heat if the colour is not dark enough. Use granulated sugar for best results.

Egg Custard — Steam egg custard over a very low heat to give it a smooth and satiny appearance. When baking a custard, stand the custard tin or dish in a pan of water. [Water should come up to half the height of the dish.] Bake in a very slow oven at 135°C–150°C (275°F–300°F). To test if custard is well-cooked, insert a skewer. If it comes out dry and clean, the custard is done.

Eggs — Use fresh eggs.

Essences — Most cakes and biscuits require flavouring. Vanilla essence is usually used but if other essences such as rose or almond are to be added, it is best to keep strictly to the measurement stated in the recipe as these essences are very strong.

Flour — Plain flour is used unless otherwise stated. Sift flour two or three times to ensure lightness.

Milk — Some recipes call for evaporated or condensed milk but fresh milk is usually used. However, powdered milk mixed with water can be substituted for fresh milk.

Sugar — Use the correct type of sugar for each recipe. Unless a certain type of sugar is specified, use castor sugar. In very few recipes do we need to use coarse or granulated sugar. Coarse or granulated sugar does not dissolve easily. When buying palm sugar it is important to get the genuine type. You can test it by pressing a tiny piece between your fingers. If the sugar turns soft and gluey it is genuine. If it feels hard and grainy it has been mixed with white sugar and is not suitable.

Yeast — Fresh yeast should be kept in the freezer and the method given in each recipe should be strictly followed.

16 Mixed Spice

30 g (1 oz) cinnamon bark
20 cloves
1 star anise
20 pieces green cardamon

1. Wash cinnamon bark, cloves and star anise. Put in the sun till very dry.
2. Remove the rounded tips from the cloves.
3. Place all the dried ingredients in a heated frying pan to fry over a low heat for 20 minutes.
4. Remove the whitish covering from the cardamon to extract the seeds.
5. Pound the spices together till very fine. Pass them through a fine sieve and store in a clean dry bottle. Keep in the refrigerator for future use.

Note:
You can heat all the dried spices in a grill pan placed under a warm grill for 10 – 15 minutes.

17 Banana Cake

455 g (16 oz) bananas
455 g (16 oz) butter
4 tablespoons condensed milk
455 g (16 oz) castor sugar
$\frac{1}{2}$ teaspoon salt
1 teaspoon banana essence
1 teaspoon vanilla essence
9 eggs
340 g (12 oz) self-raising flour, sifted

1. Mash bananas with a fork.
2. Cream butter, condensed milk and half of the sugar for 5 minutes. Add salt, banana essence and vanilla essence.
3. In a clean mixing bowl, whisk the eggs with the rest of the sugar till thick and creamy.
4. Fold in one cup of the egg mixture to the creamed butter till well mixed. Add the rest of the egg mixture, mashed bananas and lastly the flour, stirring as lightly as possible.
5. Pour into a greased cake tin. Bake in oven at 150°C (300°F) or Regulo 4 for 1–1$\frac{1}{4}$ hours.

18 Butter Cream

For a 20 cm (8 in) cake:

115 g (4 oz) butter
55 g (2 oz) sifted icing sugar
2 teaspoons rum
$\frac{1}{2}$ teaspoon vanilla essence
2 egg yolks

1. Place all the ingredients in a dry mixing bowl.
2. Beat at moderate speed for about 7–8 minutes till mixture turns to a smooth cream.
3. Chill in refrigerator until ready for icing and filling cake.

Note:
To make coffee-flavoured butter cream, dissolve 2 tablespoonfuls of 'instant' coffee powder in 2 tablespoonfuls of boiling water. Cool completely.
Beat into the creamed butter, continue beating for 1 – 2 minutes till well blended. Chill.

19 Pound Cake

225 g (8 oz) butter
1 teaspoon vanilla essence
3 drops almond essence
6 egg yolks
225 g (8 oz) sugar
6 egg whites with 1 teaspoon sugar

$A \begin{cases} 170 \text{ g (6 oz) flour} \\ \frac{1}{4} \text{ teaspoon salt} \end{cases}$

1. Cream butter till fluffy. Add vanilla and almond essence to blend.
2. Beat egg yolks and sugar till thick.
3. Whisk egg whites with 1 teaspoon sugar till stiff.
4. Sift A together. Mix with egg yolks and creamed butter. Fold in the egg whites and mix thoroughly.
5. Pour cake mixture into a greased cake tin and bake in slow oven at 150°C (300°F) or Regulo 4 for 1–1$\frac{1}{4}$ hours. Turn on to a rack to cool.

20 Chocolate Butter Icing

For a 20 cm (8 in) cake:

115 g (4 oz) plain chocolate, grated
½ teaspoon 'instant' coffee powder
1 tablespoon rum
115 g (4 oz) butter

1. Stir grated chocolate, 'instant' coffee powder and rum in a bowl over saucepan of simmering water till chocolate turns into a smooth cream. Remove and set aside to cool.
2. Beat butter over ice-cold water, adding the melted chocolate till mixture is of spreading consistency.
3. Spread at once on to sandwich sponge cakes or spread on to top and sides of cakes.

21 Chocolate Chiffon Cake

A {
200 g (7 oz) flour
4 level teaspoons baking powder
1 level teaspoon fine salt
}

B {
55 g (2 oz) cocoa
2 tablespoons 'instant' coffee powder
225 ml (8 fl oz) boiling water
}

370 g (13 oz) castor sugar
170 ml (6 fl oz) corn oil
8 egg yolks
1 teaspoon vanilla essence
9 egg whites
1 teaspoon sugar
1 teaspoon cream of tartar

1. Sift *A* together.
2. Blend *B* and let cool.
3. Place sifted flour and sugar in a mixing bowl. Make a well in the centre.
4. Pour the oil, egg yolks, vanilla essence and the cooled cocoa mixture into the well. Blend and beat slowly till smooth, about 5 minutes.
5. In a separate bowl, whisk egg whites with 1 teaspoon sugar and 1 teaspoon cream of tartar till very stiff, about 20 minutes.
6. Fold the egg white mixture lightly into the beaten mixture till well blended.
7. Place in an ungreased tube cake tin. Bake in a hot oven at 205°C (400°F) or Regulo 8 for ½ hour. Reduce heat to 175°C (350°F) or Regulo 6 and bake for another ¾ – 1 hour. The cake should spring back when lightly touched.
8. Invert cake and allow to cool before removing from pan.

Note:
Sift in the cream of tartar to the egg whites while whisking to mix it evenly.
Pre-heat oven before use.

22 Cherry Cake

170 g (6 oz) flour
Pinch of salt
1 teaspoon baking powder
255 g (9 oz) butter
200 g (7 oz) sugar
5 eggs
1 teaspoon vanilla essence
55 g (2 oz) cherries, sliced
4 cherries, cut into halves

1. Sift flour, salt and baking powder.
2. Cream butter and sugar till light and fluffy. Add eggs, one at a time, beating well after each egg. Add the vanilla essence.
3. Mix flour with the sliced cherries and fold into the creamed mixture.
4. Pour cake mixture into a greased cake tin and bake in moderate oven at 175°C (350°F) or Regulo 6 for 1·0 minutes.

Note:
Place the halved cherries on top of the cake after it has been baked for 10 minutes in the oven. This will prevent the cherries from sinking into the cake.

23 Christmas Cake

A {
225 g (8 oz) raisins
225 g (8 oz) sultanas
225 g (8 oz) currants
115 g (4 oz) lemon and orange peel
}

B {
170 g (6 oz) flour
115 g (4 oz) self-raising flour
1 teaspoon mixed spice*
$\frac{1}{4}$ teaspoon fine salt
1 teaspoon bicarbonate of soda
}

85 g (3 oz) almonds, blanched and chopped coarsely
55 g (2 oz) cherries, sliced
225 g (8 oz) butter
225 g (8 oz) fine sugar
Grated rind of one lemon
6 eggs, beaten till creamy
2 tablespoons brandy

1. Chop *A* coarsely. Sift *B* together.
2. Rub the chopped fruits, almonds and cherries with the sifted flour in a bowl. Set aside.
3. Cream the butter, sugar and rind of lemon till light. Add the beaten eggs gradually and mix well.
4. Add the flour mixed with the fruits, then the brandy and fold lightly till well mixed.
5. Grease and line a cake tin with grease-proof paper; brush paper with butter, pour cake batter in and bake in oven at 150°C (300°F) or Regulo 4 for 20 minutes. Reduce heat to 135°C (275°F) or Regulo 3. Bake until cake is done, about 45 minutes. Remove from oven.
6. Leave cake in tin for $\frac{1}{2}$ hour, before turning cake on to rack to cool. Wrap cake in tin foil. Keep for at least 3—4 days before serving.

See "Mixed Spice" on page 35.

Cherry Cake (22)

Rose Marie Cake (31)

Coffee Sponge Sandwich (24)

Coffee Walnut Cake (25)

24 Coffee Sponge Sandwich

6 eggs
170 g (6 oz) sugar
$\frac{1}{2}$ teaspoon baking powder
2 teaspoons 'instant' coffee powder mixed with 1 tablespoon hot water
$\frac{1}{2}$ teaspoon vanilla essence
115 g (4 oz) flour
55 g (2 oz) melted butter
Warm jam

1. Grease and flour two 23 cm (9 in) square sandwich tins.
2. Beat eggs, sugar and baking powder till thick and creamy. Add the coffee mixture and vanilla essence and beat till well blended.
3. Fold in the flour lightly, a little at a time. Lastly, add the hot melted butter to mix with the batter. Place in cake tins and bake in moderate oven at 175°C (350°F) or Regulo 6 for 25–30 minutes or till cake springs back at a touch of the finger. Turn cakes over on to a cooling rack. Spread cakes with warm jam or vanilla custard cream whilst still hot. Place one cake on top of the other to make sponge sandwich.

25 Coffee Walnut Cake

255 g (9 oz) flour
1 teaspoon baking powder
$\frac{1}{2}$ teaspoon salt
170 g (6 oz) chopped walnuts
225 g (8 oz) butter
200 g (7 oz) sugar
5 eggs

A {
2 tablespoons 'instant' coffee powder mixed with 1 tablespoon hot water
3 tablespoons evaporated milk mixed with 3 tablespoons water
}
1 teaspoon vanilla essence

1. Grease and flour cake tin.
2. Sift flour, baking powder and salt into a basin. Add the chopped walnuts. Set aside.
3. Beat butter and sugar till light and creamy. Add eggs, one at a time, beating well after each egg.
4. Mix A in a cup. Divide flour into three portions and fold in each portion to the creamed butter mixture each time. Lastly, add the vanilla essence. Mix lightly.
5. Pour batter into cake tin and bake in slow oven at 165°C (325°F) or Regulo 5 for 1–1$\frac{1}{2}$ hours or until cake is done. Leave cake in tin for 5 minutes and cool on a cooling rack.

26 Orange Butter Cake

200 g (7 oz) butter
200 g (7 oz) sugar
4 egg yolks
Grated rind of one orange
$\frac{1}{2}$ teaspoon vanilla essence
1 tablespoon brandy

A {
170 g (6 oz) flour
2 tablespoons milk powder
1 teaspoon baking powder
3 egg whites with 1 teaspoon sugar, stiffly beaten
6 tablespoons orange juice

1. Cream butter and sugar till light. Add yolks one at a time beating well after each addition, to prevent curdling. Beat till creamy.
2. Beat in the grated rind, vanilla essence and brandy.
3. Sift A together three times.
4. Fold in the flour, egg white and the orange juice to the creamed mixture.
5. Pour into a greased cake or loaf tin and bake in moderate oven at 175°C (350°F) or Regulo 6 for 10 minutes. Reduce heat to 150°C (300°F) or Regulo 4 for 1—$1\frac{1}{4}$ hours, or till cake is done. Leave cake in tin for 10 minutes. Turn over on to a cooling rack.

27 Ginger Cake

4 egg yolks
85 g (3 oz) sugar
85 g (3 oz) butter
55 ml (2 fl oz) black treacle
4 egg whites with 1 teaspoon sugar
$\frac{1}{2}$ teaspoon cream of tartar

A {
140 g (5 oz) flour
2 teaspoons ginger powder
$\frac{1}{2}$ teaspoon mixed spice*
1 teaspoon bicarbonate of soda

1 tablespoon brandy or rum
55 ml (2 fl oz) evaporated milk

1. Grease and flour a cake or loaf tin. Pre-heat oven to 190°C (375°F) or Regulo 7.
2. Beat egg yolks with sugar till very thick and creamy.
3. Heat butter till almost boiling, add slowly to the beaten egg yolk. Add the black treacle and beat to blend.
4. Whisk egg whites with sugar till frothy. Sift in cream of tartar and continue whisking until mixture becomes stiff and can hold its shape.
5. Sift A together three times. Combine and fold in the egg white mixture, egg yolk mixture, flour, brandy and milk. Mix well.
6. Pour into cake tin and bake in moderate oven at 175°C (350°F) or Regulo 6 for 20 minutes. Reduce oven heat to 135°C (275°F) or Regulo 3 for another 20 minutes or until cake springs back when pressed with finger. Remove and turn cake over on to rack to cool for 15 minutes.

*See "Mixed Spice" on page 35.

28 Rich Fruit Cake

A
{
285 g (10 oz) flour
1 teaspoon salt
2 teaspoons mixed spice*
}

B
{
225 g (8 oz) currants
225 g (8 oz) sultanas
225 g (8 oz) raisins
115 g (4 oz) candied peel
115 g (4 oz) almonds
115 g (4 oz) glacé cherries.
}

3 tablespoons sugar
2 tablespoons water
6 tablespoons evaporated
milk
225 g (8 oz) butter
175 g (7 oz) sugar
5 eggs, lightly beaten
1 teaspoon vanilla essence
4 tablespoons brandy

1. Sift A together. Chop B into small pieces.
2. Rub sifted flour into the chopped ingredients. Set aside.
3. Grease an 18 cm (7 in) square cake tin. Line with greaseproof paper at base and sides. Grease paper.
4. Caramelize the sugar and water to a dark brown. Add the evaporated milk and stir over a low heat to dis-solve the caramel. Cool in refrigerator.
5. Cream butter and sugar till light. Add beaten eggs a little each time and beat till well blended.
6. Add the vanilla essence, caramel and 2 tablespoons of the flour to the egg mixture. Beat lightly till well blended.
7. Fold in the remaining flour-fruit mixture and the brandy. Stir well.
8. Pour batter into cake tin and bake in oven at 175°C (350°F) or Regulo 6 for $1-1\frac{1}{4}$ hours or till cake is done. Leave cake to cool in tin before turning out on to a cake rack.

Note:
Fruit cake will taste better if it is kept for at least 3–4 days. Wrap cake in tin foil and keep in an airtight container.

*See "Mixed Spice" on page 35.

29 Rich Butter Cream

170 g (6 oz) sugar
2 tablespoons water
2 egg yolks
115 g (4 oz) butter
$\frac{1}{2}$ teaspoon vanilla essence

1. Boil sugar and water till it turns into a thick syrup. Set aside to cool for a minute.
2. Whisk egg yolks. Stir in the syrup gradually. Continue whisking till mixture is well-blended. Chill in refrigerator for 20 minutes.
3. Cream butter, and beat into the egg mixture, a little at a time. Beat in the vanilla essence.
4. Continue whisking until well-blended.
5. Store in a plastic container in a refrigerator.

30 Rich Butter Cake

310 g (11 oz) flour
10 egg whites
310 g (11 oz) sugar
2 teaspoons baking powder
10 egg yolks, lightly beaten
455 g (16 oz) butter
6 tablespoons condensed milk
2 drops almond essence
2 teaspoons vanilla essence
2 teaspoons brandy

1. Sift flour twice.
2. Beat egg whites, sugar and baking powder till thick. Add the beaten egg yolks, a little at a time, and continue beating till thick and creamy. Remove to a basin.
3. Place butter and condensed milk in a mixing bowl. Beat till well blended, about 5 minutes. Add almond and vanilla essence and brandy. Beat till blended.
4. Add one cup of egg mixture and mix thoroughly. Fold in flour lightly with the rest of the beaten egg mixture. Pour batter into a greased cake tin and bake in moderate oven at 175°C (350°F) or Regulo 6 for 10 minutes. Reduce heat to 135°C (275°F) or Regulo 3 and bake for a further 45—50 minutes or till done. Turn cake on to a cake rack.

To make Rich Marble Cake:

1. Set aside one-third of the cake mixture in a bowl. Sift 2 tablespoons cocoa and stir lightly into the mixture.
2. Pour and spread half of the white batter into a greased cake tin.
3. Place and space out small heaps of the cocoa mixture over batter in tin.
4. Add the rest of the white cake mixture to cover the cocoa mixture completely. Bake as for Rich Butter Cake.

31 Rose Marie Cake

20 egg yolks
170 g (6 oz) sugar
340 g (12 oz) butter
1 teaspoon vanilla essence
6 egg whites beaten with 1 tablespoon sugar

A {
85 g (3 oz) flour
170 g (6 oz) Marie biscuits, finely pounded and sifted
$1\frac{1}{2}$ teaspoons baking powder
$\frac{1}{2}$ teaspoon mixed spice*
}

1. Beat egg yolks with 85 g (3 oz) of the sugar till thick and creamy.
2. Cream butter with the remaining sugar till fluffy. Beat in the vanilla essence.
3. In a clean and dry bowl, whisk egg whites and 1 tablespoon sugar till stiff, but not dry.
4. Sift A. Fold the sifted ingredients, egg yolks and whites into the creamed mixture.
5. Pour mixture into a greased cake tin and bake in oven at 150°C (300°F) or Regulo 4 for 15 minutes. Reduce heat to 135°C (275°F) or Regulo 3 and bake for another $\frac{3}{4}$—1 hour or till cake is done.

*See "Mixed Spice" on page 35.

455 g (16 oz) butter
225 g (8 oz) semolina
12 egg yolks
5 egg whites
255 g (9 oz) sugar
140 g (5 oz) flour
$\frac{1}{2}$ teaspoon mixed spice*

A
4 tablespoons brandy
3 drops almond essence
1 teaspoon vanilla essence
3 drops rose essence
225 g (8 oz) almonds, chopped
coarsely

1. Beat butter for 15 minutes; add the semolina and continue beating for another 10 minutes. Leave in bowl to stand for 4 hours.
2. Beat egg yolks, whites and half of the sugar together till creamy. Add the rest of the sugar and beat till very thick.
3. Sift flour and mixed spice twice.
4. Mix creamed butter and semolina with 225 ml (8 fl oz) of the egg mixture and A till well blended. Then fold in the flour and the chopped almonds alternately with the rest of the egg mixture.

5. Pour into a greased tin and bake in a very slow oven at 135°C (275°F) or Regulo 3 for 1–1$\frac{1}{2}$ hours. Test cake to see if it is done, i.e. when it springs back at a touch or when cake shrinks from sides of tin. Turn on to a cooling rack.

Note:
Mix the chopped almonds with the sifted flour before folding in to the creamed mixture.

*See "Mixed Spice" on page 35.

200 g (7 oz) sugar
8 eggs
2$\frac{1}{2}$ tablespoons evaporated milk
1 teaspoon vanilla essence
130 g (4$\frac{1}{2}$ oz) flour

1. Grease and flour two Swiss roll tins.
2. Beat sugar and eggs till very thick and creamy. Add evaporated milk and vanilla essence. Beat till well blended.
3. Fold flour lightly into egg mixture. Pour cake mixture into tins. Bake in a hot oven at 205°C (400°F) or Regulo 8 for 7 minutes.
4. Turn cakes on to a damp towel and roll with the towel. Leave for a minute, unroll and spread with jam. Roll again. Cool before cutting into pieces.

34 Walnut Cake

140 g (5 oz) butter
170 g (6 oz) fine sugar
3 eggs and 1 egg yolk
A { 115 g (4 oz) self-raising flour
    55 g (2 oz) plain flour
B { 4 tablespoons evaporated
      milk
    4 tablespoons milk
170 g (6 oz) finely chopped
    walnuts
    Butter cream or warm jam

1. Cream butter and sugar till light and fluffy.
2. Add eggs, one at a time, beating well after each egg.
3. Sift A together. Mix B together.
4. Fold the flour, milk and walnuts lightly into the egg mixture.
5. Pour batter into two greased sandwich tins already dusted with flour. Bake in a moderate oven at 175°C (350°F) or Regulo 6 for 20–30 minutes.
6. Cool cakes in tins for 5 minutes before turning them on to a wire rack.
7. Sandwich the two cakes with rich butter cream or warm apricot jam.

35 Rich Chocolate Cake

200 g (7 oz) Cadbury's dark
    chocolate
A { 225 g (8 oz) 'soft as silk' flour
      (White Wings brand)
    2 teaspoons baking powder,
      heaped
    $\frac{1}{4}$ teaspoon bicarbonate of
      soda
    55 g (2 oz) Cadbury's cocoa
10 eggs, separated [each egg
    to weigh approx. 85 g (3 oz)]
285 g (10 oz) castor sugar
1 teaspoon bicarbonate of
    soda
310 g (11 oz) butter
$\frac{1}{2}$ tin condensed milk
2 teaspoons vanilla essence
2 tablespoons brandy

1. Break chocolate into small pieces. Place in a small enamel basin to be melted over a pan of simmering water. Cool.
2. Sift A three times.
3. Beat egg whites with half of the sugar till frothy; add 1 teaspoon bicarbonate of soda and continue beating till stiff but not dry.
4. Beat butter and the remaining sugar till light and fluffy. Add the condensed milk by spoonfuls and the melted chocolate. Beat to blend.
5. Add egg yolks, one at a time, to the creamed mixture; beating well after each addition. Add the vanilla essence and brandy and beat till well blended.
6. Add the beaten egg whites; mix well, add the sifted flour. Stir till well blended. Pour batter into two well-greased round tins 25 cm (10 in) diameter by 7·5 cm (3 in) deep and bake in oven at 175°C (350°F) or Regulo 6 for 20–25 minutes or till cake springs back when lightly pressed with the finger. Remove from oven.
7. Turn cakes on to a cake rack to cool completely before icing.
8. Spread with butter or chocolate icing to sandwich cakes then spread icing on top and sides of cake.

Note:
Pre-heat oven before use.
See "Chocolate Butter Icing" on page 37.

BISCUITS,

PIES,

AND

PASTRIES

Pineapple 'Open' Tarts (50), Pineapple-shaped Tarts (51), Spritches Butter Biscuits (39), Almond Oat Biscuits (36), Melting Moments (43), Deep-fried Bananas (94), Rich Chocolate Cake (35), Beef Curry Puffs (52), Chocolate Eclairs (48), Cream Puffs (48).

Helpful Hints for Biscuits, Pies, and Pastries

Most recipes on pies and pastries call for butter and margarine. For puff pastry it is best to use a special pastry margarine which is available at supermarkets. It makes the pastry flaky, light and easy to handle.

To make an even and round pie crust, roll a piece of dough into a ball. Flatten it with the palm of your hand. Using a floured rolling pin, roll out from the centre to the edge, keeping pastry circular. Shape to the correct size to fit the dish or tin. Allow a 2·5 cm (1 in) margin of rolled-out pastry to the size of pan or pie-dish. Do not stretch pastry when lining the inside of pan or pie-dish.

To prevent pie shell from shrinking when baking, do not roll the dough too thinly. Roll evenly and allow it to settle for a while in pan. Pat out all air and prick the bottom and sides of pie shell thoroughly. Do not stretch pastry.

Pastry improves with chilling in the refrigerator. Brush the bottom and sides of pie shell with beaten egg white before you put in the filling to prevent it from oozing out. Bake in a very hot oven.

To glaze:

For a shiny golden brown glaze, brush with milk or beaten egg yolk to which a pinch of sugar and a pinch of salt have been added or egg yolk with 1 tablespoon melted butter and a pinch of salt.

Snip the top of pie shell to allow the steam to escape. Roll and cut pastry patterns of leaves and roses, etc. Brush with water and paste on to pie to decorate. Glaze before baking.

Pastry dough can be made and stored in the freezer. Roll and bake as required. Baked pastry shells kept in an airtight container should keep for a week or two.

*   *   *   *

36 Almond Oat Biscuits

140 g (5 oz) butter
140 g (5 oz) granulated sugar
1 tablespoon self-raising flour
225 g (8 oz) quick cooking oats
55 g (2 oz) chopped almonds
2 drops of almond essence
1 teaspoon vanilla essence

1. Cream butter and sugar till light and fluffy. Add the other ingredients and mix well.
2. Pinch small portions of the mixture [each the size of a quail's egg]. Flatten lightly with finger tips.
3. Space biscuits out on a greased baking tray. Bake at 150°C (300°F) or Regulo 4 for $\frac{1}{2}$ hour or till light brown.
4. Cool on a wire rack before storing.

Note:
Decorate with chopped almonds.

37 Almond Raisin Rock Cookies

225 g (8 oz) self-raising flour
$\frac{1}{2}$ teaspoon mixed spice*, optional
 Pinch of salt
2 teaspoons baking powder
85 g (3 oz) butter, chilled
115 g (4 oz) sugar
55 g (2 oz) chopped almonds, roasted
55 g (2 oz) raisins
2 eggs lightly beaten with 1 teaspoon vanilla essence

1. Sift flour, spice, salt and baking powder into a bowl.
2. Rub butter into flour mixture till it resembles breadcrumbs.
3. Combine the flour, sugar, almonds, raisins and the beaten eggs to form a soft dough. Do not rub or knead.
4. Space dough out in small heaps on a greased tray and bake in a moderate oven at 150°C (300°F) or Regulo 4 for 20–25 minutes until brown.
5. Cool on a wire tray.

*See "Mixed Spice" on page 35.

38 Butter Almond Oat Biscuits

140 g (5 oz) butter
115 g (4 oz) sugar
1 tablespoon treacle or golden syrup
115 g (4 oz) self-raising flour, sifted
$\frac{1}{4}$ teaspoon salt
170 g (6 oz) quick-cooking oats
55 g (2 oz) chopped almonds
55 ml (2 fl oz) boiling water with 1 teaspoon bicarbonate of soda

1. Cream butter, sugar and syrup till fluffy. Mix in the flour, salt, oats, and almonds.
2. Dissolve bicarbonate of soda in the boiling water. Add to the creamed mixture and mix to form a stiff dough. Chill in refrigerator for $\frac{1}{2}$ hour.
3. Divide dough into small portions. Roll each portion into a walnut-sized ball, flatten a little and place on a greased tray leaving space to spread well. Bake in oven at 150°C (300°F) or Regulo 4 for 20 – 30 minutes till light brown.
4. Cool and store in an airtight container.

39 Spritches Butter Biscuits

910 g (32 oz) plain flour
455 g (16 oz) 'Maizina' brand flour
455 g (16 oz) butter
455 g (16 oz) icing sugar
8 egg yolks
2 teaspoons vanilla essence
4 egg whites and 1 teaspoon sugar

1. Sift the two types of flour together into a basin.
2. Beat butter, sugar and egg yolks to a cream. Add vanilla essence and mix.
3. In a separate bowl, whisk the egg whites with 1 teaspoon sugar until thick.
4. Mix the creamed butter mixture with the flour and the whisked egg whites to form a soft dough.
5. Press dough through a biscuit pump using any design. Space biscuits out on a greased tin and bake in moderate oven at 150°C (300°F) or Regulo 4 for 25–30 minutes, or till light golden brown. Cool on rack before storing in an airtight container.

Note:
Beat egg whites in a very clean and dry mixing bowl.

40 Semolina Biscuits

455 g (16 oz) flour
$2\frac{1}{2}$ teaspoons bicarbonate of soda
225 g (8 oz) ghee *or* half ghee and half butter
$\frac{1}{4}$ teaspoon almond essence
225 g (8 oz) icing sugar

1. Sift flour and bicarbonate of soda three times.
2. Soften ghee over a low heat. Remove to a bowl to cool, add almond essence.
3. Mix flour, sugar and ghee to form a soft dough.
4. Roll dough into small balls and cut each ball into halves.
5. Place on greased baking trays. Bake in oven at 135°C (275°F) or Regulo 3 for 20 – 25 minutes. Cool on a wire rack. Store in an airtight container.

41 Cat's Tongues

455 g (16 oz) flour
2 teaspoons baking powder
455 g (16 oz) butter
455 g (16 oz) sugar
2 teaspoons vanilla essence
12 egg whites beaten with 1 teaspoon sugar

1. Grease baking trays evenly with butter.
2. Sift flour and baking powder.
3. Beat butter and sugar till light and creamy. Add vanilla essence and beat till blended.
4. In a very dry and clean bowl, beat egg whites and sugar till stiff, but not dry.
5. Fold in one-quarter of the egg whites lightly to the creamed mixture. Fold in [in three parts] the flour, and the rest of the egg whites lightly to the creamed mixture.
6. Scoop batter into a forcing bag with a plain 1·3 cm icing nozzle. Press batter out in small heaps or in 5 cm lengths, 2·5 cm apart, on to greased trays.
7. Bake in oven at 150°C (300°F) or Regulo 4 for 20 – 25 minutes till pale brown. Remove from oven, take biscuits off trays immediately to cool on rack for 5 minutes. *Keep in airtight containers immediately when cool.*

Note:
Remove cat's tongues immediately from tray to cake rack after taking them out of the oven. Place them flat on a cake rack to prevent them from curling.

Right: Almond Raisin Rock Cookies (37)

Left: Cat's Tongues (41)

42 Coconut Biscuits

225 g (8 oz) self-raising flour
225 g (8 oz) plain flour
225 g (8 oz) butter
225 g (8 oz) sugar
  2 eggs
115 g (4 oz) desiccated coconut
  1 teaspoon vanilla essence

1. Sift the two types of flour together twice.
2. Cream butter and sugar till light. Add eggs, one at a time, beating lightly.
3. Stir in the flour, desiccated coconut and vanilla essence.
4. Space batter out in small heaps on greased trays and bake in oven at 150°C (300°F) or Regulo 4 till light brown.
5. Cool on a cake rack. Store in an airtight container.

43 Melting Moments

455 g (16 oz) self-raising flour
225 g (8 oz) coarse sugar
225 g (8 oz) butter
  2 eggs
115 g (4 oz) cherries, diced

1. Mix flour, sugar, butter and eggs in a large basin.
2. Mix lightly with fingertips to form a soft dough.
3. Place little lumps [each the size of a hazel nut] of the biscuit mixture on a greased baking sheet. Place a piece of cherry on top of each lump. Bake in oven at 150°C (300°F) or Regulo 4 till light golden brown for about 20 – 30 minutes. Cool on rack before storing in an airtight container.

44 Semolina Crunchies

115 g (4 oz) self-raising flour, sifted
  Pinch of salt
 55 g (2 oz) icing sugar
 85 g (3 oz) semolina
  Grated rind of one lemon
 85 g (3 oz) butter
  1 egg, lightly beaten
  2 tablespoons milk
  Egg white for glazing, lightly beaten

1. Mix and rub the flour, salt, sugar, semolina, lemon rind and butter lightly with fingertips.
2. Add the beaten egg and the milk gradually to form a dough.
3. Roll dough out on a floured board; cut with a fluted round cutter. Glaze with egg white and bake in oven at 150°C (300°F) or Regulo 4 for 20 – 25 minutes till light brown.

45 *Special Almond Biscuits*

680 g (24 oz) plain flour
170 g (6 oz) icing sugar
455 g (16 oz) butter, chilled in refrigerator
 3 egg yolks, lightly beaten with 1 teaspoon vanilla essence
 1 egg and 1 yolk, lightly beaten
115 g (4 oz) almonds, blanched and chopped coarsely

1. Sift flour and icing sugar into a basin.
2. Rub butter into the flour till mixture resembles breadcrumbs. Pour the beaten egg yolks into the flour mixture. Mix lightly to form a soft dough. Chill in refrigerator for $\frac{1}{2}$ hour.
3. Knead dough very lightly. Roll out to 0·5 cm ($\frac{1}{4}$ in) thickness on a lightly floured board or marble table top.
4. Using a fancy cutter, cut dough and place on greased baking trays. Glaze with beaten egg and sprinkle top with chopped almonds. Bake in moderate oven at 150°C (300°F) or Regulo 4 for 20 minutes. Cool on a rack and keep in an airtight container.

Note:
Divide dough into three or four portions. Flatten the dough with palm of hand before rolling out to cut. Lift dough gently with a spatula and space apart on baking trays.

46 *Sponge Fingers*

Butter for greasing
Flour for dusting
 4 egg yolks
115 g (4 oz) sugar
 1 teaspoon vanilla essence
 4 egg whites
 A pinch of salt
 2 teaspoons sugar
 85 g (3 oz) 'soft as silk' flour
 85 g (3 oz) sugar, to sprinkle over sponge fingers

1. Grease trays with butter; dust with flour.
2. Beat egg yolks and 115 g sugar till very thick and creamy. Add vanilla essence, beat till very well blended.
3. Beat egg whites till frothy; add the salt and 2 teaspoons sugar and continue beating till mixture is stiff, but not dry.
4. Lightly fold in one-third of the egg white mixture to the egg yolk mixture. Sift in one-third of the flour and stir very lightly to blend well. Repeat the process twice with the rest of the flour and the egg white and egg yolk mixture.
5. Spoon batter into a forcing bag or icing tube. Squeeze on to prepared

47 Custard Tartlets

greased trays to form finger shapes 10 cm (4 in) long and 2·5 cm (1 in) wide. Place sponge fingers 2·5 cm apart to prevent them from sticking to one another whilst being baked.

6. Sprinkle sugar over fingers and bake in oven at 150°C (300°F) or Regulo 4 for 20−25 minutes till light brown.

7. Remove fingers immediately from baking trays after taking them out of the oven. Place on cake rack to cool. Keep in an airtight container.

PASTRY:
225 g (8 oz) flour
  A pinch of salt
  2 tablespoons icing sugar
170 g (6 oz) butter
  1 egg, separated
4−5 tablespoons iced water

1. Sift flour, salt and icing sugar together.
2. Rub butter lightly into sifted flour till mixture resembles breadcrumbs.
3. Add egg yolk and water to form a dough.
4. Chill dough in refrigerator for $\frac{1}{2}$ hour. Roll dough out thinly and cut to line greased patty tins. Prick pastry with fork and brush with egg white.
5. Bake 'blind' in hot oven at 150°C (300°F) or Regulo 4 for 10 minutes.
6. Remove from oven and fill with custard.

Note:
To bake 'blind' is to bake unfilled pastry shells.

CUSTARD:
  4 eggs
  2 tablespoons condensed milk
  A pinch of salt
225 ml (8 fl oz) evaporated milk
340 ml (12 fl oz) water
  55 g (2 oz) sugar
  1 teaspoon vanilla essence
  Grated nutmeg

1. Beat eggs, condensed milk and salt lightly in a bowl.
2. Heat evaporated milk with water and sugar. Pour gradually into the egg mixture. Add vanilla essence and strain. Spoon custard into pastry cases.
3. Sprinkle with grated nutmeg and bake in oven at 150°C (300°F) or Regulo 4 for 20 − 25 minutes or until custard is firm.

48 Cream Puffs/Chocolate Eclairs

CHOUX PASTRY:

170 g (6 oz) flour
1 teaspoon baking powder
115 g (4 oz) butter
285 ml (10 fl oz) water
5 eggs

1. Pre-heat oven to 230°C (450°F) or Regulo 10.
2. Sift flour and baking powder.
3. Bring butter and water to the boil in a pan.
4. Stir in the sifted flour all at once and cook till mixture is smooth and leaves sides of pan.
5. Remove from the heat. Pour into a mixing bowl to cool. Beat in eggs, one at a time, till smooth and shiny.
6. Place cooked mixture in a forcing bag and press. Space batter out in small heaps on a well-greased tray.
7. Bake in a hot oven at 230°C (450°F) or Regulo 10 for 15 minutes. Reduce heat to 175°C (350°F) or Regulo 6 and bake for another 15 minutes till golden brown. Do not open door for the first 15 minutes when baking.
8. Cool on cake rack. Slit puffs at sides and fill with custard cream.

FILLING:

3 eggs
115 g (4 oz) sugar
3 tablespoons flour, heaped
1 teaspoon custard powder
A { 225 ml (8 fl oz) evaporated milk
{ 225 ml (8 fl oz) water
2 tablespoons condensed milk
1 teaspoon butter
1 teaspoon vanilla essence

1. Use spiral egg beater to beat eggs, sugar, flour and custard powder together in a heavy-bottomed saucepan.
2. Bring A to near boiling point.
3. Pour condensed and hot milk gradually into egg mixture. Cook mixture over a low heat, stirring all the time with egg beater till mixture is thick.
4. Remove from the heat. Stir in the butter and vanilla essence. Cool before filling.

FOR CHOCOLATE ECLAIRS:

1. Pre-heat oven to 205°C (400°F) or Regulo 8.
2. Using a large plain piping tube, pipe the Choux pastry into 7.5 cm (3 in) lengths on a lightly greased baking tray.
3. Bake for 20 – 25 minutes until golden brown.
4. Slit each eclair horizontally. Then leave to cool on a wire rack.
5. When thoroughly cold, fill with custard cream and coat the top with chocolate butter icing.*

*See "Chocolate Butter Icing" on page 37.

49 American Doughnuts

2 eggs
1 tablespoon sugar

A {
225 g (8 oz) self-raising flour
1 teaspoon baking powder
$\frac{1}{2}$ teaspoon salt
$\frac{1}{4}$ teaspoon grated nutmeg
$\frac{1}{8}$ teaspoon cinnamon powder
}

85 g (3 oz) butter
55 g (2 oz) milk
Oil for deep-frying
55 g (2 oz) icing sugar

1. Beat eggs with 1 tablespoon sugar till thick and creamy.
2. Sift A together into a bowl.
3. Rub butter into flour. Pour beaten eggs and milk into the flour mixture.
4. Mix lightly to form a soft dough.
5. Roll dough to 1 cm ($\frac{1}{2}$ in) thickness. Cut with doughnut cutter.
6. Heat oil for deep-frying. Add doughnuts and deep-fry till golden brown on both sides. Remove to absorbent paper, sprinkle with sifted icing sugar and serve hot.

Note:
Chill dough in refrigerator for 1 hour to make dough easier to handle.

50 Pineapple 'Open' Tarts

680 g (24 oz) flour
1 teaspoon fine salt
2 tablespoons fine sugar
455 g (16 oz) butter
1 egg

A {
55 ml (2 fl oz) iced water
2 teaspoons vanilla essence
3 drops of yellow food colouring
}

1. Sift flour with salt and sugar.
2. Rub butter into flour till mixture resembles breadcrumbs.
3. Beat egg lightly, add to the flour. Add A [mixed together] to form a pastry dough. Chill for $\frac{1}{2}$ hour.
4. Roll pastry to 0·5 cm ($\frac{1}{4}$ in) thickness on a floured board or marble table top.
5. Cut with a special tart cutter.
6. Fill tarts with pineapple filling.
7. Pinch a small neat frill or pattern around the edge of tart. Cut thin strips from leftover pastry to decorate top.
8. Place tarts on a greased tray and bake in a hot oven at 175°C (350°F) or Regulo 6 for 15 minutes.
9. Reduce heat and bake for another 10 – 15 minutes till light brown.
10. Turn tarts out to cool on cake rack before storing in an airtight container.

Filling: See page 56.

Note:
Use special brass pincers to pinch frill for tart.

51 Pineapple-shaped Tarts

A { 565 g (20 oz) flour
2 teaspoons baking powder
340 g (12 oz) butter, chilled

B {
2 tablespoons castor sugar
3 egg yolks
1 teaspoon vanilla essence
3 drops of yellow food colouring
$\frac{1}{2}$ teaspoon salt
8 tablespoons boiling water
Flour for dusting
Cloves

TO GLAZE:

Beat 1 egg and 1 yolk with 2 drops of yellow food colouring.

1. Sift A together into a basin.
2. Rub butter lightly into flour with tips of fingers till mixture resembles bread-crumbs.
3. Beat B lightly in a bowl.
4. Pour egg mixture into the flour mixture. Add boiling water and mix with both hands to form a pastry dough.
5. Chill in refrigerator for $\frac{1}{2}$ hour.

To shape the tarts:

1. Divide pastry into two to three parts. Place each part on a well-floured board or marble table top. Knead for a moment till smooth. Flatten pastry with palm of hand and dust with flour. Roll pastry out to 0·5 cm ($\frac{1}{2}$ in) thickness.
2. Cut pastry pieces with an oval pastry cutter.
3. Place a piece of pineapple jam on one half of the pastry and fold the other half over it. Press the edges together, using finger and thumb. Roll tart so that one end is tapered. Insert a clove [without pit] at the broad end, to resemble a pineapple stalk.
4. Using a small pair of scissors, snip tiny 'v' shapes on the front half of the tart. Snip in rows.
5. Place tarts on greased trays, leaving space for expansion. Glaze and bake in oven at 175°C (350°F) or Regulo 6 for 10 minutes. Reduce heat to 150°C (300°F) or Regulo 4 and continue baking for another 15 – 20 minutes, till light brown.

PINEAPPLE FILLING (to be made the day before):

5 pineapples, preferably Mauritian
565 g (20 oz) coarse sugar
3 cloves
1 piece 5 cm (2 in) cinnamon stick
3 segments of star anise

1. Remove skin and black eyes from pineapples.
2. Grate pineapples coarsely. Use muslin to squeeze out juice from pineapples. Do not squeeze too dry. Chop grated pineapples till fine. [Wear rubber gloves for Step 2.]
3. Place chopped pineapples, sugar, cloves, cinnamon and star anise in a heavy-bottomed aluminium sauce-pan.
4. Cook over moderate heat till almost dry, about 1 hour. Continue cooking over a low heat, till mixture is thick and gluey. Keep stirring all the while.
5. Cool. Store overnight in refrigerator.
6. Make into long rolls of 2·5 cm (1 in) diameter and cut into 1 cm ($\frac{1}{2}$ in) pieces. Roll each piece to resemble a quail's egg.
7. Place jam pieces on a tray to chill in refrigerator till ready for use.

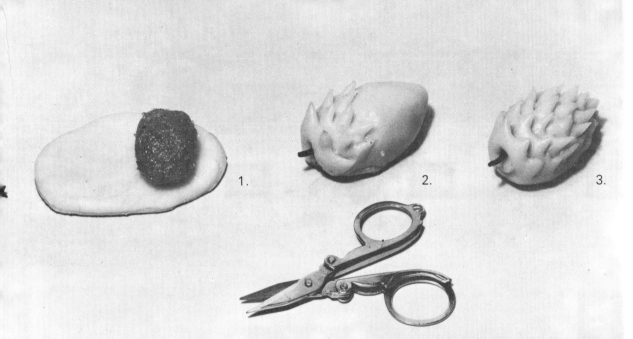

1. Place pineapple jam on one half of the pastry and fold the other half over it.
2. Snip tiny 'v' shapes on the front half of the tart.
3. Glaze and bake.

*Right: Pineapple 'Open' Tarts (50),
Pineapple-shaped Tarts (51),
Spritches Butter Biscuits (39),
Almond Oat Biscuits (36),
Melting Moments (43).*

52 *Beef Curry Puffs*

PASTRY:

225 g (8 oz) pastry margarine
1 egg
2 tablespoons castor sugar
2 tablespoons lemon juice
1 teaspoon salt
3–5 drops of yellow food colouring
170 ml (6 fl oz) iced water
455 g (16 oz) flour, sifted
115 g (4 oz) butter

1. Cut pastry margarine into 2 cm ($\frac{3}{4}$ in) cubes.
2. Mix egg, sugar, lemon juice, salt and food colouring in a bowl. Beat lightly with a fork. Pour in the iced water. Stir till well mixed. Chill in a refrigerator.
3. Place flour in a basin. Rub butter into the flour till mixture resembles breadcrumbs. Add the margarine cubes and mix lightly with the flour. Add the egg mixture and mix with both hands to form a dough. Do not knead. Chill dough in refrigerator for 1 hour.
4. Divide dough into two portions. Place one portion on a floured board or flat surface; dredge flour over; flatten and roll out into a rectangle. Fold into three, bringing down one-third of the pastry from the top to fold over the centre. Make a half turn so that the open edges on both ends face you and the fold is at your right. Roll out.
6. Repeat the folding and rolling three more times. Dust board with flour, roll out pastry to 0·5 cm ($\frac{1}{4}$ in) thickness and use a fluted-edged cutter to cut pastry into rounds.
7. Repeat process with the other portion.
8. Place a tablespoonful of filling in the centre of each round. Moisten half the edge with water and bring the other half over to seal.
9. Space curry puffs on a greased tray. Brush with glaze and bake in a very hot oven at 230°C (450°F) or Regulo 10 for 10 minutes. Bake on centre shelf of oven. Reduce heat to 205°C (400°F) or Regulo 8 and bake for another 20 minutes till golden brown. Lift curry puffs on to a wire rack to cool.

TO GLAZE:

Beat one egg with 2 drops of yellow food colouring.

FILLING:

Oil for frying
340 g (12 oz) onions, diced
340 g (12 oz) potatoes, diced
$\frac{1}{4}$ teaspoon salt
115 ml (4 fl oz) water
1 teaspoon chopped ginger
2 cloves garlic, sliced thinly
8 shallots, sliced thinly
455 g (1 lb) minced beef
4 heaped tablespoons curry powder
225 g (8 oz) grated coconut, to 125 ml (4 fl oz) water, squeezed and strained
Seasoning for curry filling:
2 tablespoons sugar
2 teaspoons salt
1 teaspoon monosodium glutamate

1. Heat an iron wok (kuali) till very hot. Add 4 tablespoons oil to heat and fry onions till transparent. Remove to a plate leaving oil in iron wok.
2. Add another 2 tablespoons oil, stir-fry potatoes with $\frac{1}{4}$ teaspoon salt over a high heat for 5 minutes. Sprinkle 115 ml water, stir and cover. Cook over a moderate heat till potatoes are cooked. Remove and set aside.

3. In a clean iron wok, heat 4 table-spoons oil to brown ginger, sliced garlic, and shallots. Add minced meat and stir-fry for 5 minutes over a moderate heat. Add the curry powder and stir-fry for another 5 minutes. Add the fried transparent onions and cooked potatoes. Mix well then add the coconut milk and the seasoning.

4. Reduce the heat, and cook till meat mixture is almost dry, stirring occasionally. Remove to a large plate to cool.

Above: Custard Tartlets (47)

BREAD

53 Danish Raisin Rolls

A {
30 g (1 oz) compressed yeast
1 teaspoon sugar
85 ml (3 fl oz) lukewarm milk
115 ml (4 fl oz) lukewarm water
2 eggs, beaten lightly
1 tablespoon flour
}

455 g (16 oz) flour, sifted twice
1 teaspoon lemon essence
115-225 g (4-8 oz) flour
225 g (8 oz) Danish pastry margarine or pastry margarine
115 g (4 oz) soft butter
225 g (8 oz) raisins or mixed fruit
Flour for dusting

1. Mix A in a bowl.
2. Stand yeast mixture in a covered bowl, in a warm place, to rise for 10 – 15 minutes.
3. Place the 455 g flour in a mixing bowl. Make a well in the centre, pour in the yeast mixture and lemon essence. Stir in the flour to form a soft dough.
4. Place dough in a greased bowl; cover with a damp cloth, and allow dough to rise in a warm place till double its bulk.
5. Knead dough on a floured board.

Add some flour, 115 – 225 g, to dough. Knead lightly till smooth. Roll dough out into a rectangle 25 cm × 30 cm (10 in × 12 in).

6. Place the whole piece of margarine in the centre of pastry and fold pastry to enclose margarine completely.

7. Use a rolling pin to flatten pastry. Then roll it out again into a rectangle.

8. Fold pastry into three, bringing down one-third from the top, to fold over the centre. Make a half turn so that the open ends face you and the fold is at your right. Roll out. Repeat the folding and rolling three more times.

9. Divide pastry into three portions. Roll out one portion into a rectangle, 23 cm × 36 cm × 0·5 cm thick (9 in × 14 in × $\frac{1}{4}$ in thick). Brush surface with one-third of the soft butter and sprinkle with one-third of the mixed fruit. Roll as for 'Swiss Roll'. Cut into 5 cm (2 in) lengths. Repeat process with the other two portions.

10. Place on greased trays, resting on cut side. Keep rolls in a warm place to rise for 20 minutes. Glaze and bake in moderate oven at 190°C (375°F) or Regulo 7 for 20 minutes till brown.

TO GLAZE:

Beat 1 egg with $\frac{1}{2}$ teaspoon salt and $\frac{1}{2}$ teaspoon sugar.

54 Sweet Corn Fritters

A {
  2 egg yolks
  1 small can whole sweet corn
  55 g (2 oz) breadcrumbs
  Pinch of salt
  Dash of pepper
  1 teaspoon baking powder
  2 egg whites
}

1. Mix A in a bowl.

2. Whip egg whites till stiff. Fold in the sweet corn mixture. Leave to stand for $\frac{1}{2}$ hour.

3. Drop spoonfuls of fritter batter into hot oil to deep-fry till golden brown or pour batter thinly into a frying pan and fry as for pancake.

55 *Buns For Braised Pork*

扣肉包

A {
  $1\frac{1}{2}$ tablespoons fresh yeast
  1 teaspoon sugar
  2 tablespoons lukewarm water
  $\frac{1}{2}$ tablespoon salt
  3 tablespoons lard or oil
}

565 g (20 oz) flour, slightly warmed under a low grill

B {
  8 tablespoons castor sugar
  225 ml (8 fl oz) lukewarm water
  Small pieces of greaseproof paper
  Flour for dusting
}

1. Dissolve *A* in a bowl and let stand for 5 minutes.
2. Place flour in a mixing bowl and make a well in the centre. Pour in the yeast mixture. Add *B* [dissolved in a bowl].
3. Stir the flour gradually to mix with the liquid to form a smooth dough.
4. Knead dough on a floured board [or use an electric dough hook] till smooth and glossy. Dough should not stick to palms of hands or inside of bowl. Place dough in a greased bowl. Cover dough with a damp cloth and leave to rise in a warm place till double its bulk.
5. Turn dough on to a floured board. Divide it into four portions. Roll each portion into a sausage and cut it into equal pieces [each the size of a hen's egg].
6. Flatten each piece with a rolling pin and shape into a round, 0·5 cm thick × 7 cm diameter. Brush half of each round lightly with oil. Fold into two and place on a piece of grease-proof paper.
7. Space buns apart on trays. Cover with a dry cloth and leave to rise in a warm place for 15 − 20 minutes.
8. Steam buns over rapidly boiling water for 7–10 minutes.
9. Serve hot with Braised Pork In Soya Sauce [See page 123].

56 *Bun Susi*

(Meat buns)

BUNS:

30 g (1 oz) or 2 tablespoons fresh yeast
3 tablespoons warm water
115 g (4 oz) castor sugar
455 g (16 oz) flour, sifted
170 ml (6 fl oz) hot milk
115 g (4 oz) soft butter
5 egg yolks
1 egg white, lightly beaten
$\frac{1}{2}$ teaspoon salt
225 g (8 oz) bread dough, from bakery
Flour for dusting

1. Dissolve yeast in 3 tablespoons warm water, 1 teaspoon sugar, and 1 tablespoon flour. Let stand for 10 minutes or till frothy.
2. Place hot milk in a mixing bowl, add the butter, egg yolks, egg white, salt, sugar, and 225 g (8 oz) of the flour. Stir till well mixed.
3. Break bread dough into small portions in a big bowl. Add the yeast mixture and the milk mixture.
4. Claw mixture with hand for 5 minutes. Add the rest of the flour to form a dough. Place dough on a flat surface and knead till dough is smooth and leaves palm of hand clean. Place dough

in a greased bowl. Cover with a damp cloth and allow to rise in a warm place till double its size.

5. Remove dough to a floured board, dust with some flour and knead for 2 minutes.

6. Divide dough into four parts and shape each into a long roll. Cut into equal walnut-sized pieces. Flatten each piece lightly with the palm of hand, making a well in the centre. Fill with meat filling and shape the dough to form a small bun.

7. Space buns out on a greased tray, allowing room for expansion. Leave to rise in a warm place for 20 — 30 minutes. Glaze and bake in oven at 205°C (400°F) or Regulo 8 for 10 minutes. Reduce heat to 150°C (300°F) or Regulo 4 and bake for a further 10—15 minutes till golden brown. Cool on a rack.

FILLING:

        3 tablespoons lard or oil
        8 shallots, sliced thinly
        1 tablespoon pounded garlic
    680 g (24 oz) minced pork
        2 teaspoons pepper
    285 g (10 oz) potatoes, diced and fried

A {
        1 teaspoon monosodium glutamate
        $\frac{3}{4}$ teaspoon salt
        3 tablespoons sugar
        2 tablespoons dark soya sauce
        4 tablespoons water
        $\frac{1}{4}$ piece grated nutmeg
        3 tablespoons crispy shallots

Thickening:
2 tablespoons cornflour with 4 tablespoons water.

1. Heat pan till very hot. Heat 3 tablespoons lard or oil to fry the sliced shallots and garlic till brown. Add the minced pork and pepper, stir-fry for 5 minutes. Add the potatoes, cook for 5 minutes.

2. Mix A in a bowl for the seasoning.

3. Pour in the seasoning, stir-fry in pan till meat mixture is almost dry.

Sprinkle with nutmeg and crispy shallots. Pour in the cornflour mixture and cook for a minute. Cool on tray before use.

TO GLAZE:
Beat 1 egg and 1 egg yolk with 1 tablespoon milk, a pinch of salt, $\frac{1}{2}$ teaspoon sugar and 2 — 3 drops of yellow food colouring.

Note:
An electric dough hook can be used to knead the dough. Use speed No 1 or No 2 for about 15 minutes or till dough leaves the inside of bowl clean.

57 *Rich Ginger Bread*

170 g (6 oz) butter
  2 tablespoons evaporated milk
140 g (5 oz) black treacle
200 g (7 oz) self-raising flour
  2 teaspoons ginger powder *or* 2
  tablespoons fresh ginger juice
  $\frac{1}{2}$ teaspoon cinnamon powder
  3 eggs and 1 egg yolk
115 g (4 oz) brown sugar
  1 teaspoon grated lemon rind

1. Heat butter, milk and treacle over a low heat.
2. Sift flour, ginger powder and cinnamon twice into a bowl.
3. Beat eggs and brown sugar till very thick and creamy. Add the lemon rind.
4. Pour the butter, milk and treacle mixture into the sifted flour and mix till well blended. Add the beaten egg mixture gradually, stirring all the time.
5. Pour into a greased loaf tin and bake on middle shelf of oven at 175°C (350°F) or Regulo 6 for 1–1$\frac{1}{2}$ hours. Cool bread in tin before turning on to a cake rack.

Note:
If fresh ginger juice is used, add it to the melted butter to cook.

Chendol (58)

DESSERTS

58 *Chendol*

(Coconut milk mix)

PEA FLOUR DROPLETS:

> **Basin of iced water**
> **10 screw pine leaves, pounded to a pulp**
> **1·2 litres (40 fl oz) water**
> $\frac{1}{4}$ **teaspoon salt**
> **1 teaspoon green food colouring**
> **1 packet green pea flour, 'Flower' brand**

1. Prepare a basin of iced water.
2. Mix the pounded screw pine leaves with the 1·2 litres water. Squeeze and strain liquid. Add the salt and food colouring.
3. Blend 225 ml (8 fl oz) of the screw pine liquid with the green pea flour in a bowl. Set aside.
4. Bring the remaining screw pine liquid to the boil in a saucepan. Remove from the heat. Stir the green pea flour mixture and pour gradually into the saucepan, stirring all the time.
5. Cook over a low heat till it boils, stirring constantly. Remove from the heat immediately when it boils. Leave to stand for 5 minutes.
6. Place the frame for making green pea flour droplets [see diagram] over the basin of iced water. Pour the hot green pea flour mixture on to the frame. Using a flat Chinese frying slice, press mixture in long, downward strokes.
7. Leave droplets to set in the iced water till firm. Add ice to the water to set droplets faster.
8. Drain in colander. Cool droplets in refrigerator till ready to serve.

PALM SUGAR SYRUP:

> **625 g (22 oz) palm sugar, grated**
> **6 tablespoons sugar**
> **225 ml (8 fl oz) water**
> **6 screw pine leaves, tied into a knot**

1. Boil all together for $\frac{1}{2}$ hour.
2. Strain syrup and set aside till ready to serve.

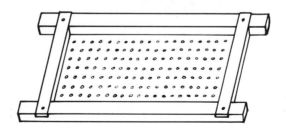

Frame for green pea flour droplets.

COCONUT MILK:

> **2 kg (4$\frac{1}{2}$ lb) grated coconut**
> **910 ml (32 fl oz) cooled, boiled water**
> **1–1$\frac{1}{2}$ teaspoons salt**

1. Add water to the grated coconut. Squeeze in small handfuls, using a piece of muslin.
2. Add salt to milk. Stir till thoroughly dissolved and cool in refrigerator.

To serve coconut milk mix:
Spoon green pea flour droplets into glasses, add some crushed ice and pour coconut milk to fill glasses. Serve with palm sugar syrup according to taste. Add salt if necessary.

[20–30 servings]

59 *Bubor Cha-cha*

(Yam treat)

905 g (32 oz) grated coconut, white
565 ml (20 fl oz) cooled, boiled water
   for No 2 milk
310 g (11 oz) diced sweet potatoes
310 g (11 oz) diced yam
225 ml (8 fl oz) water
   6 screw pine leaves, tied into a
   knot
140 g (5 oz) coarse sugar
310 g (11 oz) fine quality sago flour
   $\frac{1}{2}$ teaspoon borax, available from
   Chinese dispensaries
225 ml (8 fl oz) boiling water
   A few drops of red, green and
   blue food colouring
$\frac{1}{2}$–1 teaspoon salt

1. Squeeze grated coconut with muslin
   for No 1 milk.
2. Add the cooled, boiled water to the
   grated coconut and squeeze again
   for No 2 milk.
3. Rinse and drain sweet potato cubes,
   and steam for 5–7 minutes till cooked.
   Set aside.
4. Steam yam cubes for 5–7 minutes
   till cooked. Set aside.
5. Boil the 225 ml water with the screw
   pine leaves and sugar for 10 minutes.
   Strain syrup into a bowl.

To make sago-flour triangles:
1. Sift sago flour with the borax into
   a basin.
2. Pour the boiling water over the sago
   flour. Stir with a wooden spoon to
   combine.
3. Knead to form a firm dough. Flour
   palms of hands with sago flour to
   prevent dough from sticking to them.
   Knead dough till smooth.
4. Divide dough into four parts. Leave
   one part uncoloured. Mix a few drops
   of different food colouring to the
   other three parts. Knead till colour
   blends in.
5. Roll each part into thin long strips
   of about 1 cm in diameter. Use
   a pair of scissors to cut each strip
   into small triangles.
6. Bring a saucepan of water to the boil.
   Place the sago triangles in the boiling
   water, stirring to keep them from
   sticking together. Scoop out the
   cooked sago triangles as soon as
   they float to the surface. Soak them
   in a basin of cold water for 10 minutes.
7. Drain and place in a bowl. Add 4
   tablespoons sugar and mix to keep the
   cooked sago triangles separated.

To boil the coconut milk:
1. Mix syrup with No 2 coconut milk
   in a saucepan. Bring to the boil over
   a low heat, stirring all the time.
2. Pour in the No 1 milk and add salt.
   Stir well. Cook for a moment.
   Remove from the heat and keep
   stirring for a while to prevent mixture
   from curdling and turning oily.

To serve:
Place a tablespoonful each of cooked
sweet potatoes, yam, and sago triangles in
a small bowl. Add coconut milk to fill
the bowl. Serve hot or cold.

Note:
*Clean yam with a brush. Wipe it dry and remove
the dark skin. Do not wash after removing the
skin or it will be very slimy and difficult to
handle. Keep diced yam dry.*
*Place saucepan of boiled coconut milk in a
large basin of cold water and stir to release
the heat to prevent curdling when cooking in
big amounts.*

60 *Lotus Seed Fluff*

腐竹，蓮子，雞蛋，糖水

3·2 litres (112 fl oz) water
55 g (2 oz) pearl barley, washed and drained
115 g (4 oz) gingko nuts, blanched and skinned [remove centre sprouts]
Dried, wrinkled soya bean strips [see notes on preparation]
6 screw pine leaves
510 g (18 oz) sugar
8–10 eggs, beaten with 4 tablespoons water and 1 tablespoon sugar
Lotus seeds [see notes on preparation]

1. Bring water to the boil. Add the pearl barley and gingko nuts. Boil gently for $\frac{1}{2}$ hour.
2. Add the prepared soya bean strips and screw pine leaves and let simmer for $\frac{1}{2}$ hour. Add the sugar and cook for 10 minutes.
3. Increase heat to high. Pour in the beaten egg mixture gradually, stirring till egg floats to the surface. Remove from heat. Lastly, add the prepared lotus seeds. Remove screw pine leaves. Serve hot.

Note:
To serve as a cold dessert, let cool completely and then chill in the refrigerator.
[Serves 25 bowls]

To prepare dried, wrinkled soya bean strips:
170 g (6 oz) dried, wrinkled soya bean strips
1·4 litres (48 fl oz) cold water
$\frac{1}{2}$ teaspoon bicarbonate of soda

1. Soak soya bean strips in cold water for 10 minutes. Add bicarbonate of soda, mix and allow to soak for 20 minutes.
2. Rinse and soak again in cold water. Drain just before use.

To prepare dried lotus seeds:
115 g (4 oz) dried lotus seeds, skinned
$\frac{1}{4}$ teaspoon bicarbonate of soda
595 ml (21 fl oz) cold water to boil lotus seeds
2 screw pine leaves
115 g (4 oz) sugar

1. Soak lotus seeds in cold water for 20 minutes. Split lotus seeds and remove green centres, if any.
2. Add bicarbonate of soda and allow lotus seeds to soak for 3 hours.
3. Rinse and drain lotus seeds and bring to the boil with 340 ml (12 fl oz) of the cold water and two screw pine leaves. Let simmer for $\frac{1}{2}$ hour. Add remaining cold water and 115 g sugar and cook for another 10 minutes. Do not stir after sugar has been added. Remove from the heat and set aside. Remove screw pine leaves.

61 Talam Agar-agar

(Frosted agar-agar)

BOTTOM LAYER:

30 g (1 oz) agar-agar, soaked and cut into small pieces

1·4 litres (48 fl oz) water

6 screw pine leaves, tied into a knot

395 g (14 oz) coarse sugar

A few drops of red food colouring

3 drops of rose essence

1. Press soaked agar-agar lightly to fill one cup.
2. Boil the water and screw pine leaves in a saucepan. Dissolve agar-agar in it. Add sugar and boil till dissolved.
3. Remove from the heat. Stir in the red food colouring and the rose essence.
4. Rinse a round cake tin, 28 cm in diameter and 5 cm deep. Pour the agar-agar into the tin. Allow to set 20—30 minutes, till a thin film forms over the surface, before pouring in the coconut layer.

COCONUT LAYER:

680 g (24 oz) grated coconut, white

1 litre (36 fl oz) water

4 screw pine leaves, tied into a knot

30 g (1 oz) agar-agar, soaked and cut into small pieces

85 g (3 oz) coarse sugar

$\frac{1}{2}$ teaspoon salt

1. Squeeze grated coconut for No 1 milk. Set aside 340 ml (12 fl oz).
2. Boil the water and screw pine leaves in a saucepan. Dissolve the agar-agar in it. Add sugar and boil till dissolved.
3. Reduce the heat to low, pour the No 1 milk gradually into the saucepan, stirring well into the agar-agar mixture. Add salt, stir until it comes to a boil.
4. Remove mixture to a jug and very gently pour it in, from the side of cake tin, over the red layer, allowing it to run and spread over the surface.
5. Allow to cool and set on a flat surface. Chill in refrigerator. Cut and serve.

Note:
Do not shake or move the tray of agar-agar until it is well set.

62 Almond Jelly

1 handful of agar-agar strips

510 ml (18 fl oz) water

4 tablespoons sugar

455 ml (16 fl oz) fresh milk

1 tablespoon condensed milk

3 drops of almond essence

1. Soak agar-agar strips in cold water, squeeze out water. Cut agar-agar into very small pieces. Press lightly to fill half a 225 ml (8 fl oz) measuring cup.
2. Boil the water and dissolve the agar-agar in it. Add sugar and boil till dissolved.
3. Pour in the fresh milk and condensed milk. Stir and cook for 2 minutes. Remove from the heat. Add almond essence.
4. Pour into a rinsed jelly mould to set. Cool and chill in refrigerator.

To serve almond jelly:
Place jelly in a deep bowl, add canned longans or lychees and cherries with the syrup. Add chipped ice and serve.

Talam Agar-agar (61)

Groundnut Creme (63)

Almond Jelly (62)

Baked Caramel Egg Custard (64)

63 Groundnut Creme 花生糊

625 g (22 oz) groundnuts, shelled
2 tablespoons rice, washed and drained
2 litres (72 fl oz) water
310 g (11 oz) sugar

1. Roast groundnuts till light brown and remove skin.
2. Using an electric blender, blend rice and half of the groundnuts with 455 ml (16 fl oz) water till very fine. Add two or three tablespoonfuls of water if necessary to keep the mixture moving and rotating. Pour into a bowl and set aside.
3. Repeat process using the other half of the groundnuts with another 455 ml water.
4. Place the blended groundnuts, sugar and remaining water in a heavy-bottomed aluminium saucepan. Bring to the boil over a moderate heat. Stir mixture all the time with a wooden spoon. Let simmer for 5 minutes, stirring continuously. Remove from the heat. Serve hot or cold.

Note:
Do not allow the groundnut mixture to stick to the bottom of pan.

64 Baked Caramel Egg Custard

CUSTARD:
4 eggs, large
570 ml (20 fl oz) milk *or* 285 ml (10 fl oz) evaporated milk with 285 ml (10 fl oz) water
2–4 tablespoons sugar
A pinch of salt
1 tablespoon condensed milk
1 teaspoon vanilla essence

1. Beat eggs lightly with a fork.
2. Place milk, sugar, salt and condensed milk in a saucepan. Bring to the boil then remove from the heat. Add vanilla essence.
3. Pour the milk mixture gradually into the beaten eggs. Stir and strain custard into a basin.
4. Line mould with caramel and pour custard into mould. Stand the mould in an oven-proof dish containing cold water and bake in oven at 135°C (275°F) or Regulo 3 for 1–1¼ hours until set.

CARAMEL:
115 g (4 oz) sugar
8 tablespoons water

1. Boil the sugar and water in a saucepan. Stir sugar in pan till dissolved. Let liquid boil, without stirring, till light brown.
2. Remove from the heat. Pour caramel into custard mould to line base and sides. Pour custard in and bake. Serve hot or cold.

Note:
Warm mould with hot water to allow the caramel to run easily at base and sides.

65 Golden Castle Pudding

PUDDING:
115 g (4 oz) butter
115 g (4 oz) sugar
3 eggs
140 g (5 oz) self-raising flour, sifted
4 tablespoons evaporated milk
1 teaspoon vanilla essence

1. Beat butter and sugar till creamy. Add eggs one at a time. Beat till fluffy. Fold in the sifted flour.
2. Add the milk and vanilla essence, stir to blend. Pour into a greased pudding basin or small jelly moulds. Cover with greaseproof paper or tin foil and steam over rapidly boiling water for $1-1\frac{1}{4}$ hours. Serve hot or cold with chocolate sauce.

Note:
If small jelly moulds are used, fill only half the moulds. Cover and steam for 20–25 minutes.

CHOCOLATE SAUCE:
$1\frac{1}{2}$ tablespoons cocoa, dissolved in 1 tablespoon hot water
$1\frac{1}{2}$ tablespoons cornflour, dissolved in 1 tablespoon cold water
340 ml (12 fl oz) milk
4 tablespoons sugar
$\frac{1}{2}$ teaspoon vanilla essence
$\frac{1}{2}$ tablespoon butter

1. Mix cocoa and cornflour mixtures in a small saucepan.
2. Bring milk to almost boiling point. Add the sugar, stir and pour gradually into the cocoa mixture.
3. Return mixture to cook over a low heat for 2 minutes, stirring all the time. Remove from the heat, add the vanilla essence and the butter. Serve hot or cold.

66 Coconut Candy

340 g (12 oz) coarse sugar
$\frac{1}{2}$ teaspoon salt
115 ml (4 fl oz) evaporated milk with 2 tablespoons condensed milk, mixed in a cup
395 g (14 oz) grated coconut, white
1 teaspoon vanilla essence
1 teaspoon butter
A few drops of food colouring

1. Place sugar, salt and milk in an aluminium wok (kuali) and cook over a low heat till sugar is dissolved. Stir constantly.
2. Add the grated coconut. Stir and cook till almost dry, about $\frac{1}{2}$ hour. Remove from the heat, add vanilla essence, butter and mix.
3. Divide into portions and add drops of different food colouring if desired.
4. Fill greased trays with coconut candy. Press candy down firmly with a plastic sheet and allow to cool. Turn out candy and cut before it is completely dry and hardened. Cool completely before storing.

67 *Ice Cream*

A
{
One can of condensed milk
One big can of evaporated milk
1 teaspoon salt
910 ml (32 fl oz) hot water
}

B
{
1 heaped teaspoon gelatine, dissolved in 115 ml (4 fl oz) boiling water and cooled
1 heaped teaspoon custard powder blended with 2 tablespoons water
3 yolks, lightly beaten
One big can of creamed corn
1 tablespoon vanilla essence
}

1. Mix *A* and *B* in separate bowls.
2. Place milk mixture in a heavy-bottomed saucepan. Bring to the boil over a low heat, stirring occasionally. Remove from the heat.
3. Pour 225 ml (8 fl oz) of this hot milk slowly into the custard mixture. Add the remaining milk mixture, stir to blend.
4. Return mixture to the saucepan and bring to a boil, stirring all the time, over a low heat. Remove and pour mixture into a large basin to cool completely.
5. Add the creamed corn and the vanilla essence. Stir well. Freeze in an ice cream tub, an electric ice cream freezer or in freezer trays.

Using an ice cream tub:
4.5 kg (10 lb) coarse salt
9 – 11 kg (20 – 25 lb) ice, in chunks

1. Pour the ice cream mixture into the ice cream can, cover and secure top of can with the handle for churning.
2. Put ice chunks and salt, in alternating layers, around can, till they come up to three-quarters of can.
3. Turn the handle of tub to churn till the mixture starts to freeze and set, about 20 minutes. Drain the water from the tub through a hole at the side.
4. Place more ice and salt around can. Continue churning till the mixture is frozen hard. Remove lid to check.
5. Tilt tub slowly to let water out. Pack more ice and salt around can. Cover tub with a thick towel and leave to freeze for 1 hour. Remove can from tub to serve ice cream.

Using an electric ice cream freezer:
Use as instructed by manufacturers.

Using trays:
Pour ice cream mixture into trays. Freeze till almost set. Remove and put into an electric blender. Turn control to low and beat till well blended. Pour back into trays and freeze till set.

68 *Cocoa Custard*

COCOA CUSTARD

A {
- 140 g (5 oz) cornflour
- 2 tablespoons fresh milk
- 4 tablespoons undiluted evaporated milk
- 225 ml (8 fl oz) water

B {
- 2 tablespoons cocoa powder
- 3 tablespoons hot water

625 ml (22 fl oz) boiling water
2 egg whites, stiffly beaten

1. Mix A and B in separate bowls.
2. Combine both mixtures in a thick-bottomed aluminium saucepan.
3. Add the boiling water gradually, stirring all the time.
4. Boil mixture over a low heat until it thickens, stirring constantly. Add the beaten egg whites and break them up roughly. Cook for $\frac{1}{2}$ minute. Pour custard into a rinsed mould to set. Cool in refrigerator and serve with vanilla sauce.

VANILLA SAUCE

A {
- One big can of evaporated milk
- 455 ml (16 fl oz) water
- 4 tablespoons condensed milk
- $\frac{1}{2}$ teaspoon salt
- 7 tablespoons sugar

B {
- 1 tablespoon custard powder
- 1 tablespoon water
- $\frac{1}{2}$ teaspoon salt

2 eggs, lightly beaten
1 teaspoon vanilla essence
1–2 teaspoons rum or brandy

1. Mix A and B in separate bowls.
2. Place milk mixture in a saucepan and cook over a low heat, stirring continuously till nearly boiling. Remove.
3. Mix beaten eggs and custard mixture together. Add 225 ml (8 fl oz) of the hot milk. Stir till well blended.
4. Pour this egg mixture gradually into the remaining milk in saucepan, stirring well.
5. Cook over a low heat for 5–7 minutes, stirring occasionally. Remove from the heat, cool for a while and add the vanilla essence and rum or brandy. Serve hot or cold with the cocoa custard.

SINGAPORE FAVOURITES

Sop Kambing (178)
Mee Goreng (73)

75

69 *Mee Siam*

(Rice vermicelli with spicy gravy)

RICE VERMICELLI:

A {
225 g (8 oz) shallots
50–60 dried chillies
2 tablespoons shrimp paste
}

340 ml (12 fl oz) oil
3 tablespoons dried prawns, pounded finely

B {
400 ml (14 fl oz) water
1 tablespoon salt
3 tablespoons sugar
1 teaspoon monosodium glutamate
}

1·2 kg (43 oz) bean sprouts, washed and drained
625 g (22 oz) rice vermicelli, soaked in a saucepan of boiling water for $\frac{1}{2}$ minute and drained

1. Pound A to a fine paste.
2. Heat a large iron wok (kuali). Heat the oil. Fry dried prawns for a minute. Add paste (Step 1) and fry till fragrant and oil comes through. Set aside 3 tablespoonfuls of this fried paste and some oil for the gravy.
3. Add B and bring to the boil.
4. Add the bean sprouts and stir-fry for a minute. Push bean sprouts to one side of the wok. Add rice vermicelli and stir-fry over a high heat, using a pair of chopsticks, till gravy is absorbed.
5. Mix bean sprouts and rice vermicelli together thoroughly. Reduce the heat, stir and cook till rice vermicelli is dry and fluffy. Remove to cool on a large tray.

GRAVY:

A {
8 tablespoons preserved soya beans, pounded finely
6 tablespoons sugar
2 onions, sliced thinly
2 walnut-sized tamarind with 225 ml (8 fl oz) water, squeezed and strained
1·8 litres (64 fl oz) water
}

1. Place A in a saucepan. Stir and bring to the boil. Let simmer for $\frac{3}{4}$ hour.
2. Add the 3 tablespoonfuls of fried paste and oil. [Rice vermicelli, Step 2]. Boil for 5 minutes. Remove from the heat. Serve hot.

SPICY PASTE (SAMBAL):

40 g dried chillies *or* 10 tablespoons chilli paste
1 teaspoon shrimp paste
8 tablespoons oil
1 onion, chopped finely
1 teaspoon salt
2 teaspoons sugar
1 tablespoon tamarind with 125 ml (4 fl oz) water, squeezed and strained

1. Grind dried chillies with shrimp paste till very fine.
2. Heat an aluminium wok (kuali). Heat oil and fry chopped onion till soft and slightly brown. Add chilli paste (Step 1) and fry over a moderate heat till fragrant and oil comes through.
3. Add salt, sugar, and half of the tamarind water. Stir-fry for a minute, add the rest of the tamarind water and cook for another 2 minutes, stirring all the time. Remove to a bowl. Serve with the rice vermicelli.

Mee Siam

GARNISH:

　12 hard-boiled eggs, cut into wedges
　　or sliced

　　4 big soya bean cakes, diced and
　　　fried

625 g (1 lb 6 oz) medium-sized prawns
　　[shelled and deveined], fried and
　　halved lengthwise

115 g (4 oz) chives cut into 2·5 cm
　　(1 in) lengths

310 g (11 oz) local limes, cut into
　　halves

To serve:

Place rice vermicelli on a large serving
plate or on individual dinner plates.
Garnish and serve with the gravy and the
spicy paste.

[12 servings]

70 *Poh Pia*

(Shredded bamboo shoot rolls)

FILLING:

A {
905 g (2 lb) streaky pork
A pinch of salt
1 litre (40 fl oz) water

455 g (1 lb) small prawns
225 ml (8 fl oz) lard or oil
8 tablespoons pounded garlic [about 30 cloves]

B {
8 tablespoons preserved soya beans, pounded
1–1½ tablespoons salt
8 tablespoons sugar
2 teaspoons monosodium glutamate

1·8 kg (4 lb) Chinese turnip, shredded
1·8 kg (4 lb) boiled, tender, bamboo shoots; shredded
12 soya bean cakes cut into thin strips and fried

To cook filling:

1. Boil *A* for ¾ hour. Remove pork and slice thinly. Slice again into fine strips. Set aside 455 ml (16 fl oz) of the stock.
2. Shell and devein prawns. Pound prawn shells; add 1 litre water. Strain and set aside liquid.
3. Heat an iron wok. Heat lard and fry garlic till light brown. Add *B*. Stir-fry for a minute. Pour in the prawn liquid (Step 2) and bring to the boil.
4. Add turnip and cook for a while. Add the bamboo shoots and the pork stock (Step 1) and bring to a rapid boil. Boil for ½ hour over a moderate heat.
5. Lower heat, add fried soya bean strips and sliced pork. Cook for 1½ hours, stirring occasionally. Add the prawns and cook for a further 10 minutes.
6. Remove filling to an aluminium saucepan. Simmer until ready to serve.

WHITE SKINS:

625 g (22 oz) white skins, large

1. These skins can be bought.
2. Keep white skins covered with a damp cloth before serving.

EGG SKINS:

A {
285 g (10 oz) flour
A pinch of salt
3 tablespoons cornflour

10 eggs
680–740 ml (24–26 fl oz) water
85 ml (3 fl oz) oil

To make egg skins:

1. Sieve *A* into a basin.
2. Beat eggs lightly in a bowl. Add water and oil.
3. Make a well in the centre of the flour. Add the egg mixture and stir the flour to mix evenly. Pass mixture through a wire strainer and leave to stand for 20 minutes.
4. Grease a well-heated omelette pan. Pour enough batter to spread over base of pan thinly, as for a pancake. Cook till pancake leaves sides of pan. Turn pancake over on to a flat surface. Repeat process until batter is used up. Pile egg skins on a plate.

GARNISH:

A {
    8 eggs
    A pinch of salt
    3 tablespoons oil
}

B {
    455 g (1 lb) small prawns, shelled and deveined
    A pinch of salt
}

905 g (32 oz) cucumber, shredded thinly and with centre and skin removed

905 g (32 oz) bean sprouts; picked, washed and scalded

8 bundles of fine Chinese parsley [roots removed], washed and drained

455 g (16 oz) green lettuce, washed and drained

225 g ($\frac{1}{2}$ lb) steamed crab meat

2 pairs of Chinese sausages, fried and sliced thinly

285 g (10 oz) sweet, thick, black, sauce

30 cloves garlic, pounded to a fine paste

30 cloves garlic, pounded and fried till crisp

455 g (16 oz) red chillies, pounded to a fine paste

1. Beat *A*. Grease pan lightly. Fry egg mixture thinly as for pancakes. Roll egg pancakes and slice very thinly. [Grease pan only once.]

2. Fry *B*. Slice prawns lengthwise.

To serve shredded bamboo shoot rolls:

1. Place small heaps of cucumber, bean sprouts, Chinese parsley, and lettuce on an oval serving plate.

2. Arrange crab meat, prawns, egg, and sausages on a round plate.

3. Place the sweet, thick black sauce, garlic, fried garlic, and pounded chillies in small separate bowls.

4. Arrange the white skins and the egg skins on two separate plates.

5. Place the filling in a deep large bowl.

To roll:

1. Place a white or egg skin on a plate and spread ingredients in this order — a little sweet, thick black sauce, pounded chillies, and pounded garlic.

2. Add a piece of lettuce, a few strands of bean sprouts, shredded cucumber, and a spoonful of filling.

3. Garnish with a few slices of Chinese sausages, egg, prawn, and crab meat. Add a little Chinese parsley, sprinkle a bit of crispy garlic and fold into a neat roll.

4. Cut and serve.

Note:

1. *You need to grease the omelette pan only once as the mixture has sufficient oil.*

2. *Dip shredded Chinese turnip in water to remove the starch. Drain in a colander before cooking.*

3. *Drain gravy from filling before serving.*

[Serves 12–15 people]

79

71 *Mee Rebus*

(Noodles with beef and prawn gravy)

A {
18 slices galangal
4 cloves garlic
115 g (4 oz) shallots
14–20 dried chillies
$\frac{1}{2}$ thumb-sized piece turmeric
1 teaspoon shrimp paste
}

B {
680 ml (24 fl oz) water
1 chicken cube
225 g ($\frac{1}{2}$ lb) beef shin, cut into small pieces
}

225 g ($\frac{1}{2}$ lb) small prawns, shelled
115 ml (4 fl oz) oil
910 ml (32 fl oz) water

C {
115 g (4 oz) preserved soya beans, pounded
1 teaspoon monosodium glutamate
1–1$\frac{1}{2}$ tablespoons salt
2 tablespoons sugar
}

D {
115 g (4 oz) boiled sweet potatoes, mashed finely
2 tablespoons flour
2 tablespoons cornflour
225 ml (8 fl oz) water
}

680 g (24 oz) fresh yellow noodles
565 g (20 oz) bean sprouts, washed and picked

1. Grind A to a paste.
2. Boil B over a low heat till meat is tender.
3. Fry prawn shells with 1 tablespoonful of the oil for a minute. Remove. Bring the 910 ml water to boiling point. Add fried shells and let water boil for 7 minutes. Strain and set aside the stock for the gravy.
4. Heat an aluminium wok. Heat the rest of the oil and fry A (Step 1) till it smells fragrant, 5–7 minutes. Add C. Stir and remove the paste.
5. Place the prawns, prawn stock, B (Step 2) and the fried paste in a saucepan. Bring to the boil.
6. Thicken 225 ml of this gravy with D. Pour it back gradually into the saucepan and stir. Let gravy simmer for 10 minutes. Serve with the noodles and bean sprouts.

GARNISH:

8 sprigs Chinese celery, cut into small pieces
4 soya bean cakes, diced and fried
10 green chillies, sliced
6 red chillies, sliced
55 g (2 oz) crispy shallots*
12–14 local limes, halved
6 hard-boiled eggs, sliced

To prepare and serve noodles:

1. Bring a saucepan of water to a rapid boil.
2. Scald a handful of noodles and some bean sprouts in the boiling water.
3. Use a wire-mesh ladle to drain and remove noodles and bean sprouts to a plate.
4. Spoon some simmering gravy, prawns, and beef over noodles. Garnish. Serve hot.

*For crispy shallots, see "Helpful Hints".

[10 servings]

Left: Mee Rebus (71)

Right: Braised Hot Pot (72)

72 *Braised Hot Pot*

卤鷄翅

565 g (20 oz) water convolvulus
20 dried bean curd cakes
6 tablespoons lard or oil
8 slices ginger
3 tablespoons pounded garlic

A {
6 pieces salted bean curd in oil, mashed
4 tablespoons preserved soya beans, pounded
4 tablespoons sugar
2 tablespoons ginger juice
8 tablespoons sweet red sauce
}

B {
$\frac{1}{2}$ tablespoon salt
2 tablespoons light soya sauce
1 teaspoon monosodium glutamate
}

455 ml (16 fl oz) water
455 g (1 lb) chicken wings
455 g (1 lb) lean streaky pork
455 g (1 lb) pig's skin, cleaned and cut into 10 cm (4 in) square pieces
455 g (1 lb) small intestines of a pig
2 large cuttlefish, soaked in alkaline water* and quartered

1. Wash and scald the water convolvulus. Drain and knot each strand.
2. Scald the dried bean curd cakes. Drain and squeeze lightly to remove the oil.
3. Heat a large iron wok (kuali). Heat lard and fry ginger slices and garlic till light brown. Add A and half of the sweet red sauce. Stir-fry over a moderate heat till the sugar dissolves.
4. Add B and 225 ml (8 fl oz) of the water. Bring to the boil.
5. Add the chicken wings, streaky pork, pig's skin and small intestines. Cook for 20 minutes.
6. Remove chicken wings to a dish.
7. Add the rest of the water and the remaining sweet red sauce.
8. Add the water convolvulus, dried bean curd cakes and cuttlefish. Boil gently for 5 minutes. Remove to a dish.
9. Let gravy simmer till pork, pig's skin and small intestines are tender. Add hot water to gravy if necessary.
10. Return the chicken wings, water convolvulus, dried bean curd cakes, and cuttlefish to the gravy. Let simmer until ready to serve. Serve steaming hot in a pot with chilli sauce and sweet red sauce in separate saucers.

Note:
Buy cuttlefish that has been soaked in alkaline water from any market. Pork and chicken livers can be added to this dish.

*For alkaline water, see page 30.

73 *Mee Goreng*

(Fried noodles — Indian-style)

Oil for frying
1 onion, sliced finely
2 tomatoes, cut into wedges
225 g (8 oz) Chinese cabbage
    cut into 5 cm (2 in) lengths
455 g (16 oz) bean sprouts
340 g (12 oz) fresh yellow
    noodles

A {
2 – 3 tablespoons tomato sauce
1 – 2 tablespoons light soya
    sauce
4 – 8 tablespoons paste for
    noodles
4 green chillies, sliced
4 red chillies, sliced
4 small potatoes; boiled,
    skinned and cut into
    wedges
}

4 eggs
    Sprinkling of light soya
    sauce
2 tablespoons crispy shallots*
6 small local limes, halved

1. Heat an iron wok (kuali) till smoky. Put in 2 tablespoons oil, and fry onion slices till soft and transparent. Add the tomatoes, Chinese cabbage and toss in wok. Add bean sprouts and noodles and stir for a minute.

2. Mix in A. Toss mixture in wok till well mixed.

3. Push noodles to one side of wok. Add 2 tablespoons oil and scramble eggs [two at a time] with a sprinkling of light soya sauce. Mix egg and noodle mixture together thoroughly. Add paste for noodles [see below] according to taste. Stir and toss mixture over a very high heat for a minute. Remove to a serving plate.

4. Garnish with crispy shallots, and local limes.

PASTE FOR NOODLES:

A {
225 g (8 oz) onions
55 g (2 oz) dried chillies
4 cloves garlic
1 tablespoon shrimp paste
}
340 ml (12 fl oz) oil
55 g (2 oz) dried anchovies

B {
1 tablespoon sugar
1 teaspoon salt
1 teaspoon monosodium glutamate
}
285 ml (10 fl oz) water

1. Grind A till fine.

2. Heat 115 ml (4 fl oz) oil in pan; fry anchovies over a moderate heat till crisp. Drain and pound anchovies coarsely.

3. In a clean pan, heat remaining oil. Stir in A (Step 1) and fry till fragrant and oil comes through. Add B. Lower the heat; add the pounded anchovies. Cook for 2 – 3 minutes, remove to a bowl. Use as required. Store the remainder in a freezer.

Note:
Fry noodles over a very high heat to keep the bean sprouts crunchy and to prevent the noodles from being soggy. Fry in two parts if the wok is not large enough.

For crispy shallots, see "Helpful Hints".

[8 servings]

74 *Otak-otak Panggang*

(Spicy fish grilled in banana leaves)

A {
2 onions, weighing 225 g (8 oz)
30 slices galangal [weighing approx. 85 g or 3 oz]
6 candlenuts
25 dried chillies
1 tablespoon shrimp paste
1 thumb-sized piece turmeric
}

1·2 kg (2 lb 11 oz) Spanish mackerel
170 ml (6 fl oz) water
A pinch of salt
680 g (24 oz) grated coconut [extract 285 ml (10 fl oz) No 1 milk]
2 eggs

B {
3 tablespoons sugar
2 tablespoons salt
1 teaspoon monosodium glutamate
3 tablespoons oil
2 teaspoons roasted coriander
}

2 lime leaves, sliced very finely
4 turmeric leaves, sliced very finely
26 banana leaves (22 cm × 20 cm or 10 in × 8 in), washed and scalded

1. Grind A to a fine paste.
2. Bone and fillet the fish. Use a spoon to scrape half of the meat into a bowl. Slice the other half thinly.
3. Pound or mince the scraped fish meat till smooth. Add the water and salt. Beat mixture manually till it forms a sticky paste.
4. Add the No 1 milk. Beat till well-blended. Add the eggs, A (Step 1) and B and beat till well-blended. Add the sliced fish, lime leaves and turmeric leaves. Mix well into the fish mixture.
5. Place 2 tablespoonfuls of fish mixture in the middle of each banana leaf. Wrap to form a neat oblong, 8 cm × 10 cm (3 in × 4 in). Fasten the two ends of the leaf with a stapler or a sharp toothpick.
6. Pre-heat grill till very hot. Place wrapped fish in grill pan, 8 cm (3 in) from the hot grill, for 7–10 minutes on each side. [Wrapped fish can also be cooked in an ungreased hot iron wok.]

Using an electric blender:

1. Blend A (Step 1) with part of the No 1 milk till fine, adding further spoonfuls of milk to keep the mixture moving.
2. Add the pounded fish meat and blend for a minute.
3. Add the remaining No 1 milk and B to blend. Remove to a bowl.
4. Add the rest of the ingredients. Mix well, wrap mixture in banana leaves and grill under a hot grill.

To cook spicy fish in an ungreased iron wok:

Place the wrapped fish side by side in a pre-heated iron wok. Cook over a moderate heat for 10 minutes on each side. This is almost similar to grilling over a charcoal fire. It gives the fish a sweet aroma, keeps it moist and makes it tastier than it would be if cooked under an electric grill.

75 *Chicken Rice*

CHICKEN:

A {
1·6 kg (3½ lb) whole chicken
6 – 8 cloves garlic, bashed lightly
2 thumb-sized pieces ginger, bashed lightly
4 stalks spring onions, tied into a knot
}

2·7 litres (96 fl oz) water
1 teaspoon salt

GARNISH:
2 cucumbers, sliced
4 tomatoes, sliced
2 sprigs Chinese parsley, cut into pieces

To boil the chicken:

1. Wash chicken and rub some salt over it. Stuff chicken with A.
2. Let water and 1 teaspoon salt boil rapidly over a high heat.
3. Add the chicken, cook uncovered, until water re-boils for 2 minutes. Reduce the heat to very low, cover and let simmer for 25 – 30 minutes. Do not remove lid throughout cooking time. Set aside 995 ml (35 fl oz) chicken stock for the rice. Remove chicken immediately to immerse in a basin of cold water for 5 minutes.
5. Transfer chicken to a large plate and brush it immediately with oil. Remove stuffing.
6. Allow chicken to cool before cutting it into pieces. Arrange on a serving plate.
7. Garnish. Serve with chilli sauce and ginger sauce.

RICE:
625 g (22 oz) Thai No 1 rice
115 ml (4 fl oz) lard or oil
995 ml (35 fl oz) chicken stock
2 teaspoons salt
1 teaspoon monosodium glutamate
6 screw pine leaves, tied into a knot

1. Wash rice until water runs clear. Drain.
2. Heat pan. Fry rice in heated lard for 2 minutes. Place the chicken stock, salt and monosodium glutamate in a saucepan. Add the fried rice and screw pine leaves. Boil over a moderate heat till all the stock is absorbed.
3. Reduce heat to low and cook for a further 15 minutes. Rake rice with a fork and serve hot.

GINGER SAUCE:

2 thumb-sized pieces ginger

A {
55 ml (2 fl oz) chicken stock
½ teaspoon salt
½ teaspoon monosodium glutamate
½ teaspoon sugar
}

1. Slice ginger thinly and pound till fine.
2. Mix A in a bowl and add the pounded ginger.

CHILLI SAUCE:
10 – 12 red chillies
½ teaspoon salt
55 ml (2 fl oz) warm water
2 – 3 tablespoons lime juice

1. Scald chillies with the stems on. Remove stems and pound chillies coarsely with ½ teaspoon salt.
2. Remove to a bowl and mix with warm water and lime juice.

Note:
When cooking 625 g – 1·2 kg (22 – 43 oz) rice, use an electric rice cooker. When rice is cooked, wipe water from under the lid of cooker to prevent it from making rice soggy.
[8 servings]

*Siamese
Laksa
Lemak*

76 *Siamese Laksa Lemak*

COCKLE PASTE:

A {
4 stalks lemon grass, thinly sliced

40 – 50 dried chillies *or* 5 – 7 tablespoons chilli paste

6 red chillies, seeded

6 candlenuts

30 shallots

2 cloves garlic
}

905 g (32 oz) grated coconut

225 ml (8 fl oz) oil

B {
2 tablespoons shrimp paste dissolved in 115 ml (4 fl oz) water

2 tablespoons curry powder blended with 115 ml (4 fl oz) water

4 stalks lemon grass, bruised
}

C {
2 – 3 tablespoons salt *or* to taste

2 tablespoons sugar

1 teaspoon monosodium glutamate

10 – 20 lime leaves
}

455 g (16 oz) cockles, shelled

1. Grind *A* to a fine paste.
2. Squeeze grated coconut for No 1 milk. [Set aside grated coconut.]

3. Heat an aluminium pan. Heat oil to fry *A* and *B* till fragrant and till oil floats on top of paste.

4. Add *C* and half cup of No 1 milk. Stir-fry for a minute.

5. Remove two-thirds of paste to a dish to be used for the gravy.

6. Add cockles to the remaining paste in pan. Cook over a very high heat till done. Set aside in a dish.

GRAVY:

$$A \begin{cases} \end{cases}$$

910 ml (32 fl oz) water for No 2 milk

3·6 litres (128 fl oz) water

1 teaspoon salt

1 teaspoon monosodium glutamate

1·2 kg ($2\frac{1}{2}$ lb) whole chicken, cleaned

80 fish balls, medium-sized

40—50 spongy bean curd cubes; scalded, squeezed dry and halved

1. Add 910 ml water to the squeezed grated coconut and squeeze for No 2 milk. Set aside.

2. Boil *A* in a deep saucepan. Add chicken and boil for 7 minutes.

Cover and let simmer for $\frac{1}{2}$ hour.

3. Remove chicken and immerse it in cold water for 10 minutes. Bone the chicken and return bones to the saucepan. Boil gently for 1 hour. Strain stock. Shred chicken meat coarsely. Set aside.

4. Bring stock back to the boil and add the fish balls. Boil till fish balls float to the surface, then remove them to a dish. Set aside.

5. Add the No 2 milk, the two-thirds fried paste and bring stock back to the boil. Add the spongy bean curd cubes and the rest of the No 1 milk. Stir well. Let simmer until ready to serve.

To serve rice vermicelli:
625 g (22 oz) bean sprouts; washed, picked and scalded

One packet dried rice vermicelli, scalded and drained

GARNISH:
Boiled fish balls
Cooked chicken shreds
12 green chillies, sliced thinly
12 red chillies, sliced thinly
2 stalks phaeomaria (bunga kantan), sliced thinly
1 cup mint leaves; picked, washed and drained
10 local lemons, cut into pieces

Place a small portion of bean sprouts and rice vermicelli in a bowl. Add gravy and some spongy bean curd cubes. Add a spoonful of cockle paste and garnish. Squeeze a few drops of lemon juice before serving. Add salt to taste.

[12—15 servings]

77 *Fried Rice Noodles*

炒粿條

A {
6 tablespoons water
1 teaspoon salt
$\frac{1}{2}$ teaspoon monosodium glutamate
Lard for frying

2 teaspoons pounded garlic
310 g (11 oz) bean sprouts, washed and drained
310 g (11 oz) flat rice noodles
2 tablespoons dark soya sauce
4 eggs
4 tablespoons prepared chilli sauce *or* add to taste
1 pair of Chinese sausages, sliced thinly and fried
115 g (4 oz) cockles, shelled
55 g (2 oz) chives, cut into 5 cm (2 in) lengths
1 – 2 tablespoons sweet thick black sauce

1. Mix A in a bowl.
2. Heat a large iron wok (kuali) till smoking hot. Put in 4 tablespoons lard and fry garlic till light brown. Add the bean sprouts and rice noodles. Sprinkle A (Step 1) and the dark soya sauce and stir-fry for $\frac{1}{2}$ minute.
3. Push rice noodle mixture to one side of wok. Add 2 tablespoons lard and

scramble two eggs. Push the scrambled eggs on to the rice noodles.
4. Add another 2 tablespoons lard to scramble the other two eggs. Stir in the rice noodle mixture and mix well.
5. Pour chilli sauce over the rice noodles, add sausages, and stir-fry for another minute, adding some lard to sides of wok.
6. Make a well in the centre of mixture to put in the cockles. Cover cockles with the rice noodles, add chives and the sweet thick black sauce. Toss for $\frac{1}{2}$ minute and serve on a large serving plate.

Note:
Fry rice noodles in two parts if wok is not large enough. Fry over a very high heat to keep the bean sprouts crunchy.
Lard is preferable to groundnut oil.

CHILLI SAUCE:
1 tablespoon lard
1 tablespoon chopped garlic
$\frac{3}{4}$ teaspoon shrimp paste, crumbled

A {
285 ml (10 fl oz) liquidized chilli paste
340 ml (12 fl oz) water
$1\frac{1}{2}$ tablespoons salt
1 tablespoon sugar
1 teaspoon monosodium glutamate
1 teaspoon pepper

1. Heat lard in a small saucepan and fry garlic and shrimp paste till brown.
2. Add A and bring to the boil.
3. Boil gently for 5 minutes.
4. Cool and use as required.

Note:
Cool the chilli sauce before pouring it into a plastic container to store in the freezer.

78 *Gado-gado*

(Indonesian salad with peanut sauce)

625 g (22 oz) bean sprouts
625 g (22 oz) cabbage, diced
625 g (22 oz) long beans, cut into
 3·5 cm (1$\frac{1}{2}$ in) lengths
2·7 litres (96 fl oz) water
 1 teaspoon salt
 1 tablespoon sugar
 4 stalks lettuce; cut into 2·5 cm
 (1 in) pieces
225 g (8 oz) potatoes; boiled, peeled
 and cut into pieces
 6 soya bean cakes; fried and cut
 into pieces
 3 packets fermented soya bean
 cake; fried and cut into pieces
10 hard-boiled eggs, sliced
 Cucumber wedges

1. Boil separately: bean sprouts ($\frac{1}{2}$ minute), cabbage (5 minutes) and long beans (5 minutes) in the water with 1 teaspoon salt and 1 tablespoon sugar.
2. Lift and drain. Soak bean sprouts immediately in a basin of cold water.

SAUCE:

A {
 680 g (24 oz) roasted groundnuts, pounded
 2·3 litres (80 fl oz) water
 10 tablespoons sugar
 1$\frac{1}{2}$ tablespoons salt

B {
 15 shallots
 6 cloves garlic
 1 tablespoon shrimp paste
 20 − 30 dried chillies
 225 ml (8 fl oz) oil
 6 − 8 tablespoons vinegar
 $\frac{1}{2}$ cup crispy shallots *

1. Boil *A* for 10 minutes.
2. Grind *B* to a paste.
3. Heat an aluminium wok (kuali). Heat oil and fry paste till fragrant and oil comes through.
4. Add fried paste to the boiled groundnut sauce (Step 1). Stir, reduce the heat and let simmer for 10 − 15 minutes. Add vinegar to taste. Remove from the heat. Set aside sauce to cool. Mix in half cup of the crispy shallots.

To serve:

Arrange the lettuce on a large serving plate. Place the bean sprouts, cabbage, long beans, potatoes, soya bean cakes, and fermented soya bean cake on it. Garnish with sliced eggs and cucumber wedges. Serve with groundnut sauce separately.

For crispy shallots, see "Helpful Hints".

[12 servings]

Left: Gado-gado (78)
Below: Satay Chelop (79)

79 *Satay Chelop*

(Steamboat satay)

GRAVY:

A
- 10 candlenuts
- 140 g (5 oz) shallots
- 6 cloves garlic
- 4 stalks lemon grass, sliced
- 4 slices galangal
- 30 dried chillies
- 1 tablespoon shrimp paste

B
- 625 g (22 oz) roasted peanuts, pounded finely
- 910 ml (32 fl oz) water
- 225 ml (8 fl oz) oil

C
- 115 g (4 oz) sugar
- 1 tablespoon salt

1. Grind *A* to a paste.
2. Boil *B* over a low heat for 20 minutes.
3. Heat an aluminium wok (kuali). Heat oil. Fry paste (Step 1) in heated oil till fragrant and oil comes to surface of paste. Add fried paste to the peanut sauce. Add *C*, stir and let simmer for 10 minutes. Set aside gravy.

A
- 225 g (8 oz) rice vermicelli
- 225 g ($\frac{1}{2}$ lb) pork chop meat, sliced thinly
- 225 g (8 oz) cockles
- 225 g ($\frac{1}{2}$ lb) shelled prawns; halved lengthwise
- 225 g ($\frac{1}{2}$ lb) pork liver, sliced thinly
- 1 dried cuttlefish, soaked in alkaline water

B
- 625 g (22 oz) water convolvulus
- 455 g (16 oz) bean sprouts, picked
- 910 ml (32 fl oz) boiling water

1. Scald rice vermicelli for 2 minutes. Drain in colander.
2. Thread *A* on to wooden skewers or satay sticks.
3. Scald *B*. Drain in colander.
4. Add 225 ml (8 fl oz) of the peanut gravy to the boiling water in a small saucepan. Let simmer to cook the skewered ingredients.

To serve:

Place small servings of water convolvulus, bean sprouts, and rice vermicelli on a plate. Place the skewered ingredients in the saucepan, letting them simmer till done. Remove cooked food from skewers to the plate of rice vermicelli. Add thick gravy and serve.

[10 servings]

80 *Fried Radish Cake*

菜頭粿

A {
- **625 g (22 oz) radish**
- **910 ml (32 fl oz) water**
- **1 tablespoon salt**
- **4 tablespoons sugar**
- **1 teaspoon monosodium glutamate**

B {
- **625 g (22 oz) wet rice flour***
- **310 g (11 oz) non-glutinous plain flour**
- **910 ml (32 fl oz) water**
- **2 tablespoons oil**

1. Remove skin from white radish and grate radish finely. Place grated radish in a saucepan of cold water and bring it to the boil. Let it boil for 10 minutes, then drain. Repeat boiling process. Drain and set aside.
2. Bring *A* to the boil in a saucepan.
3. Stir *B* in a large bowl till well-blended, then pour gradually into the saucepan, stirring all the time.
4. Add the radish and oil. Reduce the heat to low. Using a wooden spoon, stir mixture till it turns thick and pasty and is only half-cooked.
5. Remove the half-cooked mixture to a square cake tin or three loaf tins, 22 cm × 8 cm × 8 cm deep ($8\frac{1}{2}$ in × 3 in × 3 in). Place tins in a steamer

to steam for $1\frac{1}{2}$ hours. Remove tins from steamer and leave radish cakes to cool in tins overnight before cutting them into pieces to fry with eggs and chilli sauce.

To fry radish cake:
- **Lard for frying**
- **8 pieces of radish cake, 8 cm square × 1 cm thick (3 in × $\frac{1}{2}$ in)**
- **4 eggs**
- **2 tablespoons dark soya sauce**
- **1 tablespoon pounded garlic**
- **2 – 4 tablespoons chilli sauce****
- **2 tablespoons sweet, thick, black, sauce**
- **2 tablespoons chopped, salted radish**
- **3 stalks spring onions, cut into 0·5 cm ($\frac{1}{4}$ in) lengths**
- **Dash of pepper**

1. Halve the ingredients. Fry each half separately.
2. To fry one half: Heat an iron wok (kuali) till smoking hot. Heat some lard to fry radish cakes on both sides till brown and slightly crisp.
3. Push radish cakes to one side of wok.

Heat 2 tablespoons lard in wok, break in eggs and spread eggs thinly in wok to cook. Mix eggs with the radish cakes. Add the dark soya sauce. Stir-fry, cutting radish cakes into pieces.

4. Push radish cake mixture to one side of wok again, add 1 tablespoon lard and fry garlic till light brown. Add 1 or 2 tablespoons chilli sauce and stir-fry with radish cake mixture for a minute. Add sweet, thick, black, sauce and salted radish with 1 or 2 tablespoons lard. Stir-fry for another 1–2 minutes. Lastly add the spring onions.
5. Remove fried radish cake to a plate, add a dash of pepper, and serve.
6. Repeat process with the other half of the ingredients.

Note:
Steamed radish cake can be kept in the refrigerator for a week. Leave to cool completely in tin first.

*See "Wet Rice Flour" on page 21.
**See "Fried Rice Noodles" on page 88.

81 Noodles In Prawn Soup

福建蝦麵

625 g (1 lb 6 oz) medium-sized
   prawns
170 g (6 oz) pork fat
   2 tablespoons oil
4·5 litres (160 fl oz) water

A {
625 g (1 lb 6 oz) pork ribs, cut
   into pieces
  1 pig's tail, cut into pieces
310 g (11 oz) lean pork
  2 teaspoons salt
  2 teaspoons sugar
  2 teaspoons monosodium
    glutamate
  1 tablespoon peppercorns
  2 tablespoons light soya
    sauce
  2 teaspoons dark soya sauce
  1 tablespoon crispy shallots*
}

455 g (16 oz) bean sprouts
310 g (11 oz) water convolvulus,
   cut into long pieces
625 g (22 oz) fresh yellow
   noodles
310 g (11 oz) rice vermicelli,
   scalded

1. Remove prawn heads. Wash and drain them.
2. Cut pork fat into small cubes and fry in pan till brown. Remove cubes and oil to a bowl.
3. In the same pan put 2 tablespoons oil. Stir-fry prawn heads for five minutes till colour turns red. Set aside prawn heads in a bowl, for the soup.
4. Boil the 4·5 litres water in a clean saucepan to cook the unshelled prawns for 2 minutes. Remove prawns to a basin of cold water. Shell and slice prawns into halves, lengthwise.
5. Return prawn shells to saucepan, add A and prawn heads. Cook over a very high heat for 10 minutes. Reduce the heat to low and let soup simmer for 1–1½ hours.
6. Strain soup. Return the bones and tail to the soup. Slice the lean pork and set aside.

GARNISH:

55 g (2 oz) crispy shallots
   Lard-oil
   Crispy cubed pork fat
   Pepper
 5 red chillies, sliced thinly
 5 green chillies, sliced thinly
   Light soya sauce

To serve:
1. Boil a saucepan of water.
2. Place a handful of bean sprouts, water convolvulus, noodles, and rice vermicelli in each medium-sized bowl.
3. Dip each serving, using a wire-mesh ladle, into the saucepan of boiling water. Drain and return to bowl.
4. Add boiling soup and a few pieces of pork ribs, tail, sliced lean pork and sliced prawns to each bowl.
5. Garnish with crispy shallots, lard-oil and crispy fat cubes. Sprinkle with pepper. Serve with a saucer of sliced chillies in light soya sauce.

Note:
Only very fresh prawns make a sweet soup.

For crispy shallots, see "Helpful Hints".

[12 servings]

82 Rice Noodles In Beef Soup

牛肉粿條

2·7 litres (96 fl oz) water
A
{
  455 g (1 lb) beef tripe, scalded
  455 g (1 lb) beef ribs
  905 g (2 lb) beef shin or brisket, whole
  1 tablespoon salt
  1 teaspoon monosodium glutamate
  1 teaspoon dark soya sauce
  1 tablespoon peppercorns
  4 cloves
  2 thick slices galangal
  1 tablespoon grated palm sugar
  1 tablespoon Bovril (optional)
}
565 g (20 oz) bean sprouts
905 g (2 lb) flat rice noodles
115 g (4 oz) salted Chinese mustard, cut into thin pieces
6 sprigs Chinese celery, cut into pieces

1. Bring water to a rapid boil in saucepan. Add A. Boil rapidly for 20 minutes.
2. Reduce heat and let simmer till meat and tripe are tender. Add Bovril to taste.
3. Remove tripe and meat from the soup and cut into small pieces.

To serve:
Boil water to scald bean sprouts. Drain. Immerse noodles in the boiling water for a moment and drain. Place a small handful of bean sprouts and noodles in a bowl, add some meat and tripe. Add boiling soup and garnish with salted Chinese mustard and Chinese celery. Serve hot with chilli sauce and pounded galangal.

Note:
Remove meat when tender and leave tripe to simmer till soft.
For pounded galangal, skin two thumb-sized pieces. Slice thinly and pound till fine.

[15 servings]

Rice Noodles In Beef Soup

83 *Satay*

(Barbecued beef with peanut sauce)

BARBECUED BEEF:

A {
- 10 shallots
- 2 cloves garlic
- $\frac{1}{4}$ thumb-sized piece turmeric *or* $\frac{1}{2}$ teaspoon turmeric powder
- 4 stalks lemon grass, sliced
- 2 slices galangal

B {
- 2 tablespoons coriander seeds
- 2 teaspoons cumin

C {
- 1 teaspoon dark soya sauce
- 1 teaspoon salt
- 4 – 5 tablespoons sugar
- 4 tablespoons oil

455 g (1 lb) beef, chilled and cut into thin pieces

1. Pound *A* to a smooth paste.
2. Fry *B* over a low heat for 5 minutes, till fragrant. Pound to a fine powder whilst still hot.
3. Mix *C* in a bowl and add to pounded paste (Step 1).
4. Rub paste mixture into the beef. Sprinkle the coriander and cumin powder over the beef and mix thoroughly. Marinate beef for 1 hour. Thread seasoned meat on to satay sticks or fine metal skewers. Grill

over a charcoal fire or under a hot grill. Baste with oil and water mixture to keep beef moist.

PEANUT SAUCE:

A {
- 15 shallots
- 8 cloves garlic
- 2 stalks lemon grass, thinly sliced
- 20 – 30 dried chillies, seeded, *or* 4 – 5 tablespoons chilli paste
- 4 thin slices galangal

455 g (16 oz) freshly roasted grounded peanuts
910 ml (32 fl oz) water
225 ml (8 fl oz) oil

B {
- 2 tablespoons salt
- 8 – 10 tablespoons sugar
- 4 tablespoons lime juice *or* 4 tablespoons thick tamarind water

1. Pound *A* to a fine paste.
2. Boil grounded peanuts with the water over a low heat till thick, stirring constantly, about $\frac{1}{2}$ hour. Set aside.
3. In a heated aluminium wok (kuali), heat the oil and fry the pounded paste (Step 1) till it smells fragrant

and the oil seeps through the paste.
4. Add this fried paste to the peanut mixture. Add *B*. Boil sauce over a low heat for 5 – 7 minutes till sugar is dissolved, stirring all the while. Cool peanut sauce and serve separately with the barbecued beef and the garnish.

GARNISH:
2 cucumbers, cut into wedges
2 onions, cut into wedges

Note:
If lemon grass is not available, use 1 teaspoon grated lemon rind.

84 *Penang Laksa*

(Fish flakes in tamarind gravy)

A {
170 g (6 oz) tamarind
4·5 litres (160 fl oz) water
455 g (16 oz) shallots
10 stalks lemon grass, thinly sliced
1 thumb-sized piece turmeric
30 – 40 pieces dried chillies *or* 4 tablespoons chilli paste
1 tablespoon shrimp paste
1 clove garlic
}

B {
8 slices dried tamarind
30 stalks polygonum (daun kesom)
2 stalks phaeomaria, (bunga kantan) cut into halves
6 heaped tablespoons sugar
2 tablespoons salt
1·2 kg (43 oz) wolf-herring, cleaned
2·4 kg (85 oz) fresh coarse rice vermicelli
6 tablespoons prawn paste, mixed with three-quarters cup warm water
}

1. Soak tamarind in 455 ml (16 fl oz) of the water; squeeze and sieve into an enamel saucepan. Repeat process three times with the rest of the water.
2. Grind *A* to a fine paste.
3. Bring tamarind water to the boil with *A* and *B*.
4. Boil for 10 minutes; add the fish and let gravy simmer for 15 minutes till fish is cooked.
5. Remove fish to a plate to cool; remove all bones. Place flaked fish meat in a bowl and set aside.
6. Let the tamarind gravy simmer for 1 hour. Remove the polygonum and phaeomaria.
7. Return the flaked fish to the gravy; bring back to the boil and serve.

GARNISH:

1 pineapple, diced
905 g (32 oz) cucumber, thinly shredded without skin and centre
55 g (2 oz) mint leaves, picked
225 g (8 oz) onions, cut into small cubes
15 green chillies, sliced
12 red chillies, sliced
115 g (4 oz) preserved leeks, sliced thinly

To serve:
1. Bring a saucepan of water to a rapid boil. Scald the rice vermicelli and drain in a colander.
2. Place a small handful of scalded rice vermicelli in a medium-sized bowl; pour hot tamarind gravy and some fish over it. Top with garnish, and 1 teaspoon of the thinned prawn paste. Serve.

Note:
Only very fresh fish is suitable for this dish. Dried coarse rice vermicelli can be substituted for the fresh rice vermicelli. Boil rice vermicelli till soft but not soggy, about 15 minutes. Rinse in cold water and drain.

Opposite: Penang Laksa

85 *Tauhu Goreng*

(Soya bean cake with peanut sauce)

A
- 3 tablespoons pounded garlic
- 10 red chillies, pounded finely
- 8 green chillies, pounded finely
- 10 – 20 'chili padi', optional, pounded finely
- 1 – 2 tablespoons dried chilli paste
- 4 – 6 tablespoons dark soya sauce
- 6 – 8 tablespoons sugar
- 4 tablespoons palm sugar, scraped
- 4 tablespoons vinegar
- 625 g (22 oz) groundnuts, roasted and grounded
- 570 ml (20 fl oz) water
- 10 big soya bean cakes, soaked in salt water and drained
- 625 g (22 oz) bean sprouts, blanched
- 625 g (22 oz) cucumber, sliced

To prepare the sauce:
1. Place A in a large bowl.
2. Add the groundnuts, half the water and blend to a smooth paste. Add the rest of the water. Stir well.

To serve:
1. Fry soya bean cakes and cut into pieces.
2. Arrange soya bean cakes on a plate, add some bean sprouts and cucumber slices.
3. Add peanut sauce and serve immediately.

[10 servings]

86 *Laksa Lemak*

(Fresh vermicelli with coconut gravy)

A
- 1 thumb-sized piece turmeric Galangal, sliced, to fill about half a teacup
- 20 dried chillies
- 5 red chillies
- 6 candlenuts
- 2 tablespoons shrimp paste
- 225 g (8 oz) shallots
- 1 tablespoon coriander powder or seeds

- 1·2 kg (43 oz) grated coconut
- 2·7 litres (96 fl oz) water for No 2 milk
- 455 ml (16 fl oz) water
- 1 teaspoon salt
- 1 teaspoon sugar
- 455 g (1 lb) fresh prawns, for garnishing
- 225 ml (8 fl oz) oil
- 2 stalks lemon grass, bruised

B
- 55 g (2 oz) dried prawns, pounded
- 1 tablespoon sugar
- 2 tablespoons salt

- 625 g (22 oz) bean sprouts, boiled and drained
- 1·2 kg (43 oz) fresh rice vermicelli

1. Grind *A* to a fine paste.
2. Using a piece of muslin, squeeze coconut for No 1 milk. Add 2.7 litres water to coconut and extract No 2 milk. Set aside.
3. Boil the 455 ml water with 1 teaspoon salt and 1 teaspoon sugar. Add fresh prawns; cook for about 5–7 minutes. Remove prawns to soak in a bowl of cold water. Shell prawns and return shells to saucepan. Boil for 10 minutes. Strain liquid for stock. [Slice prawns lengthwise. Set aside for garnishing.]
4. Heat an aluminium wok (kuali). Heat oil and fry paste (Step 1) and lemon grass till fragrant and the oil comes to the surface.
5. Add the No 2 milk and prawn stock and bring to the boil. Add *B*. Boil for 10 minutes over a low heat.
6. Reduce the heat to simmering point. Add the No 1 milk, setting aside 2 tablespoonfuls for the chilli paste. Stir gravy for a minute then remove from the heat. Continue stirring for a minute to prevent the thick coconut milk from curdling.

CHILLI PASTE:

A {
55 g (2 oz) dried chillies
5 red chillies
1 teaspoon shrimp paste
2 tablespoons oil
1–2 tablespoons water
}

B {
2 teaspoons sugar
1 teaspoon salt
2 tablespoons No 1 milk
}

1. Grind *A* to a fine paste.
2. Heat pan till hot. Heat oil and fry paste till well done and oil comes through.
3. Add 1 – 2 tablespoons water, stir-fry with *B*.
4. Remove to a bowl.

GARNISH:

Cooked prawns, shelled and sliced lengthwise

8 fish cakes, fried and sliced into thin strips

3 cucumbers, cut into thin strips without skin and centre

55 g (2 oz) polygonum (daun kesom), cut finely

To serve the rice vermicelli:
Place some bean sprouts and rice vermicelli in several bowls. Add hot gravy and garnish with prawns, fish cake, cucumber, polygonum, and chilli paste.

Note:
Transparent bean vermicelli can also be added to the rice vermicelli.

[10 servings]

SNACKS

Minced Pork and Prawn Toast (87)

87 Minced Pork And Prawn Toast

A {
225 g ($\frac{1}{2}$ lb) minced pork
225 g ($\frac{1}{2}$ lb) prawns, shelled, deveined and chopped
115 g (4 oz) canned, chopped pork with ham [mashed]
1 egg
2 small boiled potatoes, mashed
2 tablespoons chopped spring onions
$\frac{1}{8}$ teaspoon salt
1 teaspoon sugar
$\frac{1}{2}$ teaspoon monosodium glutamate
$\frac{1}{2}$ teaspoon pepper
1 big loaf of bread [French loaf], cut into 1 cm ($\frac{1}{2}$ in) thick slices
Oil for deep-frying
1 egg, beaten with a pinch of salt
}

1. Place A in a basin.
2. Mix well into a pasty mixture using a wooden spoon.
3. Spread meat mixture on to the slices of bread.
4. Heat oil for deep-frying.
5. Dip only the meat side of the bread in the beaten egg. Deep-fry over a moderate heat, meat-side down, for 2 minutes.
6. Turn over once, fry for just half a minute till light golden brown. Remove and place on absorbent paper. Serve hot with tomato sauce or salad cream.

Note:
Increase the heat just before bread is removed.

88 Cheese Toast

A {
115 g (4 oz) grated Cheddar cheese
1 tablespoon self-raising flour
}

B {
1 egg, lightly beaten
2 tablespoons evaporated milk
$\frac{1}{2}$ teaspoon pepper
Mustard to taste
}

8 slices French loaf, each about 1 cm ($\frac{1}{2}$ in) thick
Butter to spread on toast

1. Mix A in a bowl. Add B and mix thoroughly.
2. Pre-heat grill until hot. Toast bread slices till brown on both sides. Butter one side. Spread the cheese mixture on buttered side.
3. Place cheese toast under grill for 5—7 minutes or till light brown. Serve immediately.

89 *Rissoles*

(Meat rolls)

BATTER:

A {
- 170 g (6 oz) plain flour
- 2 tablespoons cornflour
- 3 tablespoons powdered milk

B {
- 6 eggs, lightly beaten
- 425 ml (15 fl oz) lukewarm water
- A pinch of salt
- 3 tablespoons oil

1. Place A in a bowl. Make a well in the centre of flour.
2. Beat B lightly with a fork and pour gradually into flour to make a smooth batter. Strain and leave batter to stand for 20 minutes.
3. Heat a 20 cm (8 in) base frying pan till very hot. Remove from the heat, grease base of pan with oil once only. Pour in batter, tilt the pan to spread batter evenly and cook. Turn pancake out when edge begins to curl and leave sides of pan. Pile pancakes on a plate.

FILLING:

- 6 tablespoons lard or oil
- 1 teaspoon garlic, pounded
- 1 onion, diced small
- 455 g (1 lb) prawns, shelled, deveined and chopped
- 455 g (1 lb) minced pork

A {
- 115 g (4 oz) steamed crab meat
- 225 g (8 oz) boiled bamboo shoots, diced
- 6 tablespoons boiled green peas
- 3 tablespoons light soya sauce
- 1 tablespoon oyster sauce
- 1 teaspoon sherry
- $\frac{3}{4}$ teaspoon salt
- 1 teaspoon monosodium glutamate
- 1 teaspoon pepper
- 2 teaspoons sugar

B {
- 1 rounded tablespoon corn-flour
- 6 tablespoons water
- 2 tablespoons spring onions, chopped finely

1. Heat oil in pan, fry garlic till light brown. Add the diced onion and stir-fry till transparent. Add the prawns and cook for a minute. Add the minced pork; stir-fry till cooked, about 5 minutes.
2. Add A. Stir well and cook over a moderate heat for 5 minutes.
3. Mix B in a bowl. Add to mixture in pan. Stir and cook for a minute. Add the chopped spring onions, stir and remove to a tray to cool.

To make rolls:

1 egg
A pinch of salt
Meat filling
'Paxo' brand golden breadcrumbs
Oil

1. Beat egg lightly with salt. Set aside.
2. Place 2 tablespoonfuls of meat filling on each pancake. Roll pancake to form a meat roll.
3. Brush roll with beaten egg and coat with breadcrumbs. Deep-fry in hot oil for half a minute over a high heat. Place rolls on absorbent paper. Serve hot or cold.

Top: Rissoles
Bottom: Steamed Radish Cake

90 *Steamed Radish Cake*

蘿蔔糕

625 g (22 oz) radish

A {
855 ml (30 fl oz) water
1 tablespoon salt
3 tablespoons sugar
1 tablespoon monosodium glutamate
}

B {
625 g (22 oz) wet rice flour*
285 g (10 oz) non-glutinous plain flour
795 ml (28 fl oz) water
}

C {
115 g (4 oz) dried streaky pork, diced
2 pairs of Chinese sausages, diced
115 g (4 oz) small, dried prawns; washed and drained .
1 tablespoon lard
}

1. Skin and grate white radish. Boil grated radish in a saucepan of water for 7 minutes. Drain and, using cold water, re-boil for another 7 minutes. Drain.
2. Place A in a saucepan and bring to the boil.
3. Mix B in a bowl. Add the boiled radish. Pour in A (Step 2) gradually, stirring all the time.
4. Transfer mixture to a heated iron wok (kuali). Lower the heat. Cook until mixture turns pasty and begins to thicken [half-cooked], stirring constantly.
5. Add C. Stir till ingredients are well mixed. Place mixture in a greased square tin and steam for 1–2 hours, or till cake shrinks a little from sides of tin. Leave to cool overnight.
6. Cut into 1 cm ($\frac{1}{2}$ in) thick pieces and fry with lard in a well-heated pan. Serve hot with chilli sauce.

*See "Wet Rice Flour" on page 21.

91 *Meat Savouries*

燒賣

A {
1 teaspoon monosodium glutamate
1 teaspoon sherry
2 tablespoons light soya sauce
½ teaspoon salt
1 teaspoon sugar
½ teaspoon sesame oil
2 teaspoons cornflour
1 tablespoon ginger juice
1 small egg
¼ teaspoon pepper
1 tablespoon chopped spring onions
}

B {
285 g (10 oz) minced pork
225 g (½ lb) prawns; shelled, deveined and cut
55 g (2 oz) boiled pork fat, finely cubed
4 tablespoons boiled bamboo shoots, chopped finely
}

115 g (4 oz) square egg skins ['wan tan' skins], obtainable from local markets

1. Mix *A* in a bowl. Add *B*. Mix well.
2. Cut off the four corners of the egg skins. Place a tablespoonful of the meat mixture in the centre of each skin. Enclose filling with egg skin, so that only the top of filling is seen. Flatten base of each meat savoury.

To steam:
Brush steamer rack with oil. Space meat savouries on rack.
Steam over rapidly boiling water for 5 – 7 minutes or till cooked.
Serve hot with chilli sauce and mustard.

[30 – 40 meat savouries]

92 *Stuffed Mushrooms*

A {
680 ml (24 fl oz) water
1 teaspoon sugar
½ teaspoon salt
1 tablespoon lard
}

225 g (8 oz) Chinese mustard
15 big Chinese mushrooms soaked in hot water
Cornflour for dusting

B {
1 egg white, lightly beaten
½ teaspoon monosodium glutamate
¼ teaspoon salt
1 teaspoon light soya sauce
1 tablespoon cornflour
Dash of pepper
1 tablespoon lard
¼ teaspoon sesame oil
}

C {
225 g (½ lb) minced pork with a little fat
455 g (1 lb) prawns, shelled, deveined and finely chopped
4 water chestnuts, finely chopped
1 tablespoon spring onions, finely chopped
}

1. Boil *A*. Add Chinese mustard, cut into pieces. Boil for ½ minute. Drain.
2. Squeeze mushrooms till dry and

remove stalks and dust underside of mushrooms with cornflour.

3. Mix *B* in a bowl. Add *C*. Mix well.
4. Spread mixture on to dusted side of mushrooms. Steam mushrooms, meat side up, on a greased plate for 7–10 minutes.

GRAVY:

$$A \begin{cases} \frac{1}{4} \text{ teaspoon salt} \\ \frac{1}{2} \text{ teaspoon monosodium} \\ \quad \text{glutamate} \\ \frac{1}{2} \text{ teaspoon sugar} \\ 2 \text{ teaspoons light soya sauce} \\ 225 \text{ ml (8 fl oz) chicken stock} \\ \quad or \text{ use } \frac{1}{2} \text{ chicken cube and} \\ \quad \text{water} \\ \quad \text{Lard for frying} \\ 1 \text{ clove garlic, finely chopped} \end{cases}$$

$$B \begin{cases} 2 \text{ teaspoons cornflour} \\ 2 \text{ tablespoons water} \end{cases}$$

1. Mix *A* in a bowl.
2. Heat 1 tablespoon lard in a hot pan. Fry chopped garlic till light brown. Pour in *A* (Step 1) and bring to the boil. Reduce heat to low.
3. Blend *B* in a bowl. Add to pan. Stir till it boils. Pour over stuffed mushrooms, arranged meat side up on the boiled mustard. Serve hot.

$$A \begin{cases} 115 \text{ ml (4 fl oz) water} \\ 1\frac{1}{2} \text{ tablespoons cornflour} \\ 1\frac{1}{2} \text{ tablespoons water chestnut} \\ \quad \text{flour} \end{cases}$$

455 g (16 oz) topside beef, minced finely

1 teaspoon alkaline water*

$$B \begin{cases} \frac{1}{4} \text{ teaspoon salt} \\ 1\frac{1}{2} \text{ teaspoons monosodium} \\ \quad \text{glutamate} \\ 3 \text{ teaspoons sugar} \\ 1 \text{ teaspoon sesame oil} \\ \text{Dash of pepper} \end{cases}$$

$$C \begin{cases} 115 \text{ g (4 oz) pork fat, cut into} \\ \quad \text{very small squares} \\ 4 \text{ sprigs Chinese parsley,} \\ \quad \text{chopped finely} \\ \frac{1}{2} \text{ teaspoon dried orange peel,} \\ \quad \text{chopped finely} \\ \text{Pepper} \end{cases}$$

1. Blend *A* in a bowl.
2. Place minced beef and alkaline water in a mixing bowl. Use hand to mix thoroughly. Slap beef on to sides of bowl. Knead till it is sticky, about 10 minutes. Leave to stand for 2 hours.
3. Transfer beef paste to a large mixing bowl. Add *A* (Step 1) and *B*. Use palms of hands to rub and knead till beef is pasty and sticky, about 10 minutes.
4. Add *C* and dash of pepper. Mix well. Grease palms of hands. Roll mixture into balls (each the size of a small egg). Place beef balls on a greased plate.
5. Steam for 10 minutes over rapidly boiling water. Serve hot.

*See page 30.

94 *Deep-fried Bananas*

Oil for deep-frying
12–14 bananas [pisang rajah],
　skinned
Plain flour for dusting

BATTER:

A {
1 teaspoon salt
1 teaspoon lime paste*
1 tablespoon lime or lemon
　juice
115 ml (4 fl oz) water
285 g (10 oz) wet rice flour**
}

1. Blend A in a cup.
2. Place flour in a mixing bowl. Add the blended mixture; mix well till batter is smooth. Let batter stand for $\frac{1}{2}$ hour.

To deep-fry bananas:

1. Heat oil in a pan for deep-frying till very hot.
2. Place bananas on a tray, dust with plain flour lightly.
3. Dip the bananas in batter and very quickly put them into the hot oil to fry till golden brown, stirring occasionally. Remove and spread on absorbent paper. Serve hot.

Note:
Do not use over-ripe bananas.
Batter is of the right consistency if it coats a spoon. Fry as many as required at one time, but oil in pan must completely cover the bananas.

*Used by betel-nut chewers.
**See "Wet Rice Flour" on page 21.

95 *Kueh Kuria*

(Tapioca doughnuts)

A {
455 g (16 oz) grated tapioca, skinned and with centre vein removed
170 g (6 oz) grated coconut, white
3 tablespoons glutinous rice flour or sago flour
$\frac{3}{4}$ teaspoon salt
}
Oil for deep frying

For the sugar coating:
55 ml (2 fl oz) water
225 g (8 oz) coarse sugar
4 screw pine leaves

1. Mix A in a bowl.
2. Form mixture into small balls, flatten, and make a hole in the centre as for American doughnuts.
3. Heat oil in iron wok (kuali) for deep-frying. Place the tapioca rings in and fry till golden brown. Remove to absorbent paper.
4. Drain oil from wok. Do not wash. Add the water, sugar and screw pine leaves. Boil till syrup is thick and sticky.
5. Reduce heat to very low and add the tapioca rings. Stir for a minute till they are well-coated with the syrup.

Remove wok from heat and keep tossing the tapioca rings in wok till the sugar is dry. Let rings cool on a rack before serving.

Note:
A thick iron wok (kuali) is recommended for frying and coating the rings because it retains the heat and dries the sugar thoroughly.

Right: Deep-fried Bananas, Kueh Kuria.

96 *Kueh Pie Tee*

(Shredded bamboo shoots in patty cases)

PATTY CASES:

A {
1 large egg, lightly beaten
225 ml (8 fl oz) water
A pinch of salt
115 g (4 oz) plain flour, sifted
Oil for deep-frying
}

1. Mix A in a bowl.
2. Pour mixture gradually into the flour to form a smooth batter. Sieve into a bowl. Leave to stand for $\frac{1}{2}$ hour.
3. Heat oil for deep-frying.
4. Heat the special patty mould in the hot oil for 2 minutes. Remove the mould, dip it in batter and deep-fry till patty case is light brown and can retain its shape when it slips away from the mould.
5. Place patty cases on absorbent paper. Cool and store in an air-tight container immediately to retain crispness.

FILLING:

455 g (1 lb) streaky pork
455 ml (16 fl oz) water
A pinch of salt

A {
1·2 kg (43 oz) tender, boiled bamboo shoots
310 g (11 oz) Chinese turnip
225 g ($\frac{1}{2}$ lb) small prawns
}

225 ml (8 fl oz) water
4 tablespoons lard or oil
2 tablespoons pounded garlic

B {
$\frac{1}{2}$ teaspoon salt
$\frac{1}{2}$ teaspoon monosodium glutamate
2 tablespoons sugar
2 tablespoons preserved brown soya beans, pounded
}

2 big soya bean cakes, cut into thin strips and fried

1. Cook pork in water and a pinch of salt for $\frac{1}{2}$ hour. Remove and slice pork thinly. Cut again into fine strips. Set aside stock.
2. Shred A finely.
3. Shell and devein prawns. Pound prawn shells. Add water. Mix well. Strain and set aside liquid.
4. Heat lard or oil in an iron wok (kuali). Fry garlic till brown, add B. Stir-fry for $\frac{1}{2}$ minute. Add shredded ingredients, prawn liquid and pork stock. Cook for $\frac{3}{4}$ hour over a moderate heat.
5. Add prawns, pork and soya bean strips. Stir and cook till almost dry. Cool on tray before filling.

GARNISH:

225 g ($\frac{1}{2}$ lb) steamed crab meat
225 g ($\frac{1}{2}$ lb) prawns, fried with a pinch of salt and cut into small pieces
3 bundles of Chinese parsley, without roots, washed and drained
4 tablespoons pounded garlic, fried crisp
2 eggs, fried into thin pancakes and shredded

To serve:

Fill patty cases with filling. Garnish. Serve with chilli sauce.

Note:
Dip shredded turnip in cold water to remove the starch. Drain in colander before cooking.

[50 – 60 patty cases]

Kueh Pie Tee

97 *Cheese Straws*

170 g (6 oz) butter
225 g (8 oz) flour

A {
225 g (8 oz) cheese, finely grated
$\frac{3}{4}$ teaspoon salt
$\frac{1}{2}$ teaspoon pepper
1 tablespoon granulated sugar
}

2 egg yolks, beaten
1 egg white, lightly beaten for glaze

1. Rub butter into flour. Add *A*. Mix well.
2. Pour the beaten egg yolks into the flour mixture. Knead lightly with hand to form a soft dough. Chill dough in refrigerator for $\frac{1}{2}$ hour.
3. Roll dough on a floured pastry board to 0·5 cm ($\frac{1}{4}$ in) thickness.
4. Cut pastry with a pastry wheel into 5 cm (2 in) blocks. Cut each block into strips, so that each strip is 5 cm long by 0·5 cm wide (2 in × $\frac{1}{4}$ in).
5. Glaze whole blocks of cheese strips with egg white. Place on baking trays and bake in oven at 190°C (375°F) or Regulo 7 for about 20 – 25 minutes till light brown. Store in an airtight container when cool.

MEAT

Beef Serondeng

98 *Beef Serondeng*

(Beef with fried grated coconut)

A {
6 slices galangal
14 shallots
4 tablespoons coriander seeds
1 teaspoon cumin seeds
4 slices ginger
3 cloves garlic
2 slices turmeric
1 teaspoon pepper
}

565 g (1 lb 4 oz) rump or Scotch steak, cut into pieces
115 ml (4 fl oz) water
6 tablespoons oil

B {
1 tablespoon salt
5 tablespoons sugar
3 tablespoons grated palm sugar
55 g (2 oz) tamarind in 8 tablespoons water, squeezed and strained
}

565 g (20 oz) coconut, white, coarsely grated

1. Pound *A* to a paste.
2. Let beef pieces simmer in 115 ml water and one-third of paste till tender and almost dry.
3. Heat 4 tablespoons oil, stir-fry remaining paste till fragrant. Add *B*, stir-fry for a minute and remove to a dish. Rub fried paste into the grated coconut.
4. Heat 2 tablespoons oil in a pan. Add the coconut mixture and the beef. Stir-fry over a low heat till moist and fragrant. Keep stirring constantly to prevent the coconut from burning.

99 *Grilled Pepper Steak*

455 g (1 lb) fillet steak

A {
1 teaspoon black peppercorns, pounded coarsely
1 teaspoon sherry
2 tablespoons oil
1 tablespoon melted butter
$\frac{1}{2}$ teaspoon monosodium glutamate
}

1. Slice steak fairly thickly.
2. Mix *A* in a bowl. Add steak to marinate for 1 hour.
3. Pre-heat grill to high. Line grill pan with foil to collect the juices for basting.
4. Place steak on heated grill rack about 5 cm (2 in) from the heat, to seal in the juices. Turn it over once. Reduce the heat to medium and grill to rare, medium or well done. Baste meat with juices whilst grilling. Serve hot with barbeque sauce, lettuce, and tomatoes.

905 g (2 lb) beef brisket, cut into pieces

A
- 1 tablespoon ginger juice
- 2 tablespoons light soya sauce
- 3 tablespoons dark soya sauce
- 1 teaspoon pepper
- 1 teaspoon monosodium glutamate

B
- 1 tablespoon sugar
- $\frac{1}{2}$ teaspoon monosodium glutamate
- $\frac{1}{4}$ teaspoon salt
- $1\frac{1}{2}$ – 2 tablespoons vinegar

C
- 1 tablespoon cornflour
- 3 tablespoons water
- 2 tablespoons lard or oil

D
- 1 tablespoon sugar
- 6 slices ginger

E
- 8 cloves garlic, lightly bashed
- 10 shallots, cut into halves

F
- 2 segments star anise
- 1 stalk lemon grass, bruised
- 2·5 cm (1 in) piece cinnamon bark

285 ml (10 fl oz) water

1. Marinate beef in *A* for 1 hour.
2. Mix *B* and *C* in separate bowls.
3. Heat lard in a hot saucepan to brown *D*. Add *E* and fry for a minute. Add *F*, marinated beef and *B* (Step 2). Stir-fry and cook over a high heat for 10 minutes. Add the 285 ml water, and let it boil for 10 minutes.
4. Transfer dish to an earthen clay pot. Bring it back to the heat and let it simmer till meat is tender, about $1\frac{1}{2}$–2 hours.
5. Thicken gravy with *C* (Step 2) and stir well.

To serve:

Place whole pieces of lettuce on a large serving plate. Arrange beef on lettuce and serve hot.

A
- 1 thumb-sized piece ginger
- 2 green chillies
- 4 cloves garlic

- 1 teaspoon salt
- 1 teaspoon monosodium glutamate

905 g (2 lb) beef [rump steak], cut into pieces

B
- 8 tablespoons curry powder
- 225 ml (8 fl oz) water
- 2 onions, thinly sliced
- 4 tablespoons ghee or oil

C
- 20 shallots, thinly sliced
- 5 cloves
- 6 cardamons, bashed
- 1 thumb-sized piece cinnamon bark

285 ml (10 fl oz) water

115 g (4 oz) grated coconut with 455 ml (16 fl oz) water, squeezed and strained

D
- 1 teaspoon salt *or* salt to taste
- 1 teaspoon monosodium glutamate
- 4 sprigs mint leaves, picked
- 2 sprigs Chinese parsley, cut finely
- 4 tomatoes, quartered

1. Pound A finely. Add salt and mono-sodium glutamate and marinate beef for $\frac{1}{2}$ hour.
2. Mix B in a bowl.
3. Heat an aluminium wok. Heat ghee to fry C till light brown. Add the marinated beef, stir-fry for 5 minutes, then add the 285 ml water. Boil gently till meat is tender, adding more water if necessary. Cook till almost dry.
4. Add B (Step 2), stir-fry over a low heat for 5 minutes with one-third of the coconut milk. Add D and the rest of the coconut milk. Let curry simmer for 15 minutes, stirring occasionally.
5. Remove from the heat. Serve hot or cold.

Note:
New potatoes can be added to the curry. Add them to cook with the mint, Chinese parsley and tomatoes.

1·4 kg (3 lb) gammon [middle cut]

A $\left\{\begin{array}{l}\text{1 large bottle of beer} \\ \text{3 segments star anise} \\ \text{2·5 cm (1 in) cinnamon stick} \\ \text{6 cloves} \\ \text{30 g (1 oz) palm sugar}\end{array}\right.$

B $\left\{\begin{array}{l}\text{2 tablespoons brown sugar} \\ \text{1 tablespoon honey} \\ \text{1 teaspoon prepared mustard}\end{array}\right.$

Juice of one orange

1 small can sliced pineapple rings, drained

1. Boil gammon with A over a moderate heat for $1-1\frac{1}{2}$ hours or till meat is tender. Leave to cool for 1 hour. Drain and remove to a roasting pan.
2. Dissolve B in the orange juice, for the glaze.
3. Remove skin from gammon. Pour the glaze over the meat and bake in a moderate heat at 175°C (350°F) or Regulo 6 for 20 minutes.
4. Remove baking pan from the oven. Place pineapple slices around the meat. Return pan to oven and bake for another 10 minutes till golden brown. Baste meat with juices from the pan from time to time.
5. Cool and store in the refrigerator if it is to be used as a cold dish.

103 Barbecued Pork Sparerib

A {
2 tablespoons tomato sauce
2 tablespoons sugar
1 tablespoon sweet chilli sauce
1 tablespoon sherry or brandy
2 tablespoons light soya sauce
$\frac{1}{2}$ tablespoon lime juice
1 tablespoon monosodium glutamate
1 teaspoon pepper
}
905 g (2 lb) pork sparerib, cut into pieces
4 tablespoons lard
4 cucumbers, sliced

1. Mix *A* in a bowl.
2. Wash the sparerib pieces. Drain and dry with a tea towel.
3. Marinate the sparerib pieces in *A* (Step 1) for 4 hours. Thread the pieces on to skewers. [Set aside marinade in a bowl for basting.]
4. Line baking tray or grill pan with foil to collect the juices and dripping for basting.
5. Heat grill or oven till very hot, 230°C (450°F) or Regulo 9–10. Brush sparerib pieces with lard. Grill or bake for 10 minutes. Turn over once to brown the other side. Reduce the heat to 150°C (300°F) or Regulo 4 and cook for another 15 – 20 minutes. Mix the dripping with the marinade. Baste and grill till well done. Serve hot or cold with cucumber slices.

104 Roast Pork Strips 叉燒

A {
1 tablespoon salt
7 tablespoons sugar
1 tablespoon light soya sauce
1 tablespoon sherry or wine
2 tablespoons monosodium glutamate
Orange food colouring
4 tablespoons water
}
905 g (2 lb) pork, cut into thick strips
3 tablespoons lard

1. Mix *A* in a bowl to marinate pork for 6 – 8 hours.
2. Thread pork on to skewers. Brush lard over pork.
3. Pre-heat grill till very hot. Grease rack with lard. Grill pork on both sides till brown. Reduce the heat to cook the pork till well done. Baste pork from time to time while grilling.

Note:
Line grill pan with foil to collect the dripping for basting. Serve with sliced cucumber.

Right: Barbecued Pork Sparerib
Roast Pork Strips

105 *Mutton Kurmah*

A $\begin{cases}\end{cases}$
1 tablespoon ginger juice
$\frac{1}{2}$ teaspoon salt
$\frac{1}{2}$ teaspoon monosodium glutamate
1 teaspoon pounded garlic

455 g (1 lb) mutton chops, cut into pieces

B $\begin{cases}\end{cases}$
4 tablespoons powdered spice [kurmah powder] for mutton chops
$\frac{3}{4}$ cup water

C $\begin{cases}\end{cases}$
170 ml (6 fl oz) evaporated milk
2 tablespoons lemon or lime juice
1 teaspoon salt
$\frac{3}{4}$ teaspoon monosodium glutamate

2 tablespoons ghee or margarine
2 onions, sliced thinly
1 green chilli, pounded finely
4 tomatoes, quartered
1 bundle of coriander leaves

1. Mix *A* in a bowl and rub into mutton chops. Marinate for 1 hour.
2. Mix *B* to a paste in another bowl. Add *C*. Add the marinated chops, mix well and set aside.

(Spicy mutton chops)

(Beef in spicy paste)

3. Heat a heavy-bottomed aluminium saucepan. Put in the ghee and fry the onions and green chilli for $\frac{1}{2}$ minute. Add the tomatoes and the chops. Do not stir. Spread coriander leaves on top.

4. Cover pan and cook over a low heat for $1\frac{1}{2}$ hours or till chops are tender. Serve hot.

On opposite page
Top: Mutton Kurmah
Bottom: Beef Rendang

A {
1 teaspoon salt
1 teaspoon monosodium glutamate
1 tablespoon sugar
1 tablespoon dark soya sauce

B {
115 g (4 oz) shallots
30 dried chillies
4 red chillies, seeded
1 clove garlic
$\frac{1}{2}$ thumb-sized piece ginger
3 stalks lemon grass, thinly sliced
4 slices galangal
5 candlenuts
1 teaspoon shrimp paste
8 tablespoons oil
2 tablespoons curry powder, mixed with 3 tablespoons water
455 g (16 oz) grated coconut with 225 ml (8 fl oz) water, squeezed and strained

C {
905 g (2 lb) rump steak, cut into pieces
1 stalk lemon grass, lightly bruised
115 g (4 oz) grated coconut, white, fried till brown and pounded to a fine paste

1. Mix *A* in a bowl.
2. Grind *B* to a fine paste.
3. Heat an aluminium wok (kuali). Heat oil and fry grounded paste and curry paste till fragrant.
4. Add half of the coconut milk and fry till oil comes through.
5. Add *A* and *C*. Stir-fry for 10 minutes. Pour in the rest of the coconut milk and let simmer till meat is tender, about 1 hour. Increase heat to reduce gravy till it is thick and oily.

107 *Braised Beef In Dark Soya Sauce*

905 g (2 lb) rump steak

A {
1 tablespoon dark soya sauce
1½ tablespoons sugar
1 tablespoon oil
2 tablespoons lard or oil
}

B {
2 slices ginger
1 clove garlic, sliced thinly
1 onion, sliced thinly
1 tablespoon sugar
5 cm (2 in) piece cinnamon bark
2 segments star anise
}

C {
½ teaspoon salt
1 tablespoon sugar
1 teaspoon monosodium glutamate
2 tablespoons dark soya sauce
1 teaspoon peppercorns
}

225 ml (8 fl oz) water

1. Marinate beef in A for 1 hour.
2. Heat lard in a heavy-bottomed saucepan. Brown B. Add the marinated beef. Increase the heat to brown beef on all sides to seal in the juices. Add C and half a cup of the water. Cook for 10 minutes. Add the rest of the water and boil for another 10 minutes.
3. Reduce the heat, cover pan and let simmer till beef is tender, about 1½–2 hours, turning beef over once in the pan. Add more water if necessary.

Note:
When beef is tender, remove the lid and increase the heat to high to thicken the sauce. Cool for a while before slicing the beef. Heat the gravy and pour over the meat before serving.

108 *Five-spice Rolls*

五香

2 dried bean curd wrappers
2 small eggs

A {
1 teaspoon salt
2 teaspoons sugar
1 teaspoon monosodium glutamate
2 teaspoons light soya sauce
1 teaspoon dark soya sauce
1 teaspoon pepper
2 tablespoons lard or oil
1 tablespoon flour
1 rounded teaspoon five-spice powder [available from Chinese medicine shops]
}

B {
455 g (1 lb) minced pork
225 g (½ lb) prawns; shelled, deveined, and chopped coarsely
1 onion, chopped finely
}

170 g (6 oz) steamed crab meat
Oil for deep-frying

1. Cut bean curd wrappers into rectangles, 15 cm × 18 cm (6 in × 7 in).
2. Beat eggs lightly. Add A. Mix well.
3. Mix B in a large basin. Add the egg mixture and mix thoroughly. Add the steamed crab meat. Mix well.

109 *Braised Mutton Ribs*

紅燒羊排骨

4. Place a small heap of this mixture on each of the wrappers. Roll as for sausages, dampen the open ends with a little flour mixed with water and seal. Steam the rolls for 10 minutes. Cool.

5. Deep-fry rolls in hot fat. Cool before cutting. Serve with cucumber slices.

565 g (1 lb 4 oz) mutton ribs, cut into pieces

A {
1 tablespoon wine or sherry
1 tablespoon light soya sauce
2 teaspoons dark soya sauce
2 teaspoons sugar
}

B {
1 tablespoon oyster sauce
1 teaspoon sugar
2 teaspoons monosodium glutamate
1 tablespoon dark soya sauce
1 tablespoon light soya sauce
}

C {
1 tablespoon cornflour
4 tablespoons water
1 teaspoon lard
}

Oil

2 tablespoons lard

D {
170 g (6 oz) boiled, tender, bamboo shoots, cut into wedges
170 g (6 oz) young tender ginger, cut into wedges
10 Chinese mushrooms, with stems removed, soaked in hot water and drained before use
}

1 tablespoon wine or sherry

225 ml (8 fl oz) water

1. Marinate ribs for $\frac{1}{2}$ hour in A.

2. Mix B and C in separate bowls.

3. Deep-fry ribs in hot smoking oil for 3 minutes. Remove and immerse fried ribs in a basin of ice-cold water. Discard the flakes of floating fat and place ribs in a dish.

4. Heat an iron wok (kuali) till very hot. Add the lard and stir-fry D for a minute. Add the ribs. Sprinkle the wine and stir-fry for another minute.

5. Pour in B (Step 2) and the water. Cook over a low heat till ribs are tender and gravy is thick and almost dry. Remove ribs to a dish.

6. Add C (Step 2), stir-fry and return ribs to cook for $\frac{1}{2}$ minute. Place on a serving plate and serve immediately.

(Meat and liver balls)

A {
4 tablespoons oil
15 shallots, pounded very finely

3 tablespoons sugar
1 teaspoon salt
2 tablespoons dark soya sauce
2 tablespoons vinegar
}

310 g (11 oz) minced pork
310 g (11 oz) pork liver, boiled, and diced very small
2 teaspoons pepper
2 tablespoons roasted coriander powder
455 g (1 lb) pork membrane, cleaned and cut into 15 cm (6 in) squares

1. Heat oil in pan and fry pounded shallots till light brown. Reduce the heat to low.
2. Add A. Stir-fry for $\frac{1}{2}$ minute. Remove pan from the heat.
3. Transfer shallot mixture to a basin. Add the minced pork and liver. Sprinkle pepper and coriander powder. Knead well with hands to mix thoroughly.
4. Take equal tablespoonfuls of meat mixture to form balls (each the size of a walnut). Place on a tray.

5. Wrap each meat ball tightly with a small piece of pork membrane. Overlap the membrane two or three times to prevent the meat from bursting out of the wrapper while being fried.

To fry meat balls:
1. Heat a flat-bottomed frying pan, half-filled with oil.
2. Place the meat balls, sealed end downwards, and fry over a moderate heat till brown. Turn over once.

Note:
1. *Boil liver till it is half-cooked. It will then bind with the minced meat and will not crumble easily.*
2. *Do not buy pig's membrane that has been kept overnight.*
3. *Wash membrane with water and remove all dirt and bristle.*
4. *Squeeze membrane lightly to drain excess water.*

A {
1 teaspoon light soya sauce
1 teaspoon dark soya sauce
1 teaspoon sherry or brandy
$\frac{1}{2}$ teaspoon oyster sauce
1 teaspoon monosodium glutamate
$\frac{1}{2}$ teaspoon pepper
$\frac{1}{4}$ teaspoon bicarbonate of soda
$\frac{1}{2}$ teaspoon sesame oil
1 teaspoon ginger juice
2 tablespoons oil
1 egg white, beaten
}

225 g (8 oz) fillet or Scotch steak, thinly sliced

B {
$\frac{1}{2}$ tablespoon cornflour
1 tablespoon oil
}

4 tablespoons lard

C {
225 g (8 oz) bean sprouts; picked, washed and drained
$\frac{1}{2}$ teaspoon pounded garlic, fried
A pinch of salt
1 teaspoon sugar
2 sprigs spring onions, cut into 5 cm (2 in) lengths
}

1. Mix A in a bowl to marinate beef for 1 hour.
2. Mix B in a bowl for the thickening.

3. Heat an iron wok (kuali) till very hot. Heat 2 tablespoons lard and stir-fry *C* for 15 seconds. Remove to a serving plate.

4. Place the other 2 tablespoons lard in wok. Stir-fry the marinated beef slices over a high heat for a minute. Add the spring onions, stir-fry and add the thickening. Mix well. Remove immediately to fried bean sprouts. Serve at once.

Top: Hati Babi Bungkus
Bottom: Sliced Beef Steak

905 g (2 lb) mutton chops, cut into pieces

A
- 2 tablespoons ginger juice
- 1 teaspoon salt
- 1 teaspoon monosodium glutamate
- 2 tablespoons curry powder
- 4 tablespoons water
- 1 tablespoon oil
- 4 tablespoons ghee *or* 2 tablespoons butter and 2 tablespoons oil

B
- 2 cloves garlic, thinly sliced
- 10 cardamons, bashed
- 8 cloves
- 1 thumb-sized piece cinnamon bark
- 2 onions, thinly sliced
- 2 tablespoons tomato ketchup
- 2 tablespoons tomato purée
- 6 tablespoons curry powder, mixed to a paste with 8 tablespoons water

455 ml (16 fl oz) water

C
- 1 teaspoon salt
- 1 teaspoon monosodium glutamate
- 2 teaspoons sugar
- 2 teaspoons lime juice

1 small can evaporated milk

1. Marinate chops in *A* for $\frac{1}{2}$ hour.
2. Heat an aluminium wok (kuali). Add ghee to brown *B*. Add sliced onions and fry till fragrant for 5 minutes. Stir in the tomato ketchup and purée.
3. Add curry paste and fry over a moderate heat till oil seeps through. Add half of the water and *C* and stir-fry for 5 minutes. Add the lime juice.
4. Add marinated chops, half of the evaporated milk, and the remaining water. Cook over a high heat for 15 minutes, stirring occasionally. Let meat simmer till tender, about $\frac{3}{4}$ hour.
5. Add the remaining evaporated milk, stir and continue simmering for another 10 minutes. Serve hot.

225 g ($\frac{1}{2}$ lb) beef fillet, sliced into bite-sized pieces

A
- 1 teaspoon dark soya sauce
- $\frac{1}{2}$ teaspoon monosodium glutamate
- $\frac{1}{2}$ teaspoon sugar
- $\frac{1}{2}$ teaspoon bicarbonate of soda
- 1 teaspoon light soya sauce
- 1 teaspoon sherry or brandy
- 1 teaspoon cornflour
- 2 tablespoons oil

B
- 1 teaspoon light soya sauce
- 1 teaspoon oyster sauce
- $\frac{1}{2}$ teaspoon sugar
- $\frac{1}{2}$ teaspoon monosodium glutamate
- $\frac{1}{4}$ teaspoon salt
- 1 teaspoon sesame oil
- 1 teaspoon sherry

C
- 2 tablespoons cornflour
- 3 tablespoons water

225 ml (8 fl oz) oil

3 tablespoons lard

D
- 4 slices ginger
- 1 teaspoon chopped garlic
- 115 g (4 oz) snow peas or French beans
- 1 green pepper, cut into small squares

扣肉

115 g (4 oz) canned button mushrooms, cut into halves
115 g (4 oz) canned straw mushrooms, cut into halves
2 stalks spring onions, cut into 5 cm (2 in) lengths

1. Marinate beef in A for $\frac{1}{2}$ hour.
2. Mix B in a clean bowl.
3. Blend C in another bowl.
4. Heat an iron wok (kuali) till smoking hot. Heat oil for deep-frying. Add the marinated beef, stir-fry for $\frac{1}{2}$ minute and remove to a plate.
5. Heat 2 tablespoons lard in a clean wok and stir-fry D over a high heat. Remove to a plate.
6. Add the mushrooms and stir-fry for $\frac{1}{2}$ minute. Add the fried mixed vegetables, fried beef, spring onions, B, and C. Stir in the last tablespoonful of lard, and mix well. Remove immediately to serve.

905 g (2 lb) pork, with skin and some fat

A {
1 tablespoon dark soya sauce
1 teaspoon honey
$\frac{1}{2}$ teaspoon five-spice powder
2 tablespoons lard

B {
2 cloves garlic, pounded finely
4 shallots, pounded finely
3 segments star anise
1 tablespoon sugar

C {
2 tablespoons dark soya sauce
1 teaspoon monosodium glutamate
1 teaspoon salt

225 ml (8 fl oz) water

1. Marinate the whole piece of pork in A for $\frac{1}{2}$ hour.
2. Heat an aluminium wok (kuali). Heat lard to fry B till light brown.
3. Reduce the heat to moderate. Add the marinated pork to brown on all sides. Add C and half of the water. Cover and cook for 10 minutes.
4. Remove the lid, turn pork over and continue boiling gently till sauce is thick and oily.
5. Add the rest of the water and bring to the boil, stirring constantly to prevent the sauce from sticking to the bottom of wok.
6. Remove meat and sauce to a heavy-bottomed saucepan. Cover and let simmer till meat is tender, $1-1\frac{1}{4}$ hours. Add a little water if sauce thickens before meat is tender. Leave to cool. Slice pork and add hot sauce. Serve hot.

115 *Satay Babi*

(Grilled or fried spicy pork slices)

225 g (8 oz) grated coconut
4 stalks lemon grass, thinly sliced
4 red chillies, seeded
10 dried chillies, seeded
4 candlenuts
1 teaspoon shrimp paste
15 shallots

B {
1 teaspoon salt
½ teaspoon monosodium glutamate
½ teaspoon pepper
2 teaspoons sugar
3 tablespoons oil
}

680 g (1 lb 8 oz) pork, cut into 1½ cm (½ in) thick slices
85 ml (3 fl oz) oil

1. Extract No 1 milk from coconut.
2. Grind *A* to a fine paste.
3. Mix the paste with *B* and the No 1 milk to season pork. Marinate for 1 hour.
4. Thread the meat on to wooden or metal skewers. Brush with oil and place under a pre-heated hot grill until cooked.

PEANUT SAUCE and GARNISH:
Please see page 95

PINEAPPLE SAUCE:

1 small ripe pineapple (preferably Mauritius pine)

1. Cut skin off pineapple and ensure the black "eyes" are removed.
2. Scrape into a bowl with a fine scraper leaving the hard core.
3. Drain off excess juice and serve the pulp in small bowls, separately or mixed with peanut sauce.

Note:
The marinated meat can also be fried over a high heat in an iron wok (kuali) till almost dry and the oil comes through. Chicken can be used instead of pork.

116 *Babi Pong Tay*

(Stewed pork)

625 g (1 lb 6 oz) pig's trotter [from the foreleg]
625 g (1 lb 6 oz) pork [from the shoulder]
6 tablespoons cooking oil

A {
115 g (4 oz) shallots, pounded coarsely
4 pieces garlic, pounded coarsely
8 cm (3 in) piece cinnamon bark
}

B {
2 tablespoons preserved soya beans, pounded
1 tablespoon sugar
1 teaspoon salt
1 teaspoon dark soya sauce
}

455 ml (16 fl oz) water

1. Cut meat into pieces.
2. Heat an iron wok (kuali). Heat oil and brown *A*. Add *B* and stir-fry for ½ minute.
3. Add the meat. Add one-third of the water and cook over a high heat, stirring occasionally till almost dry, about ½ hour.
4. Pour in the remaining water and bring to a rapid boil for 5 minutes. Transfer the stewed pork to a heavy-bottomed aluminium saucepan, cover and let

simmer for $1-1\frac{1}{2}$ hours or till meat is tender. Serve hot or cold.

Note:
This is an ideal picnic dish eaten with French loaf. Add more hot water when meat is tender, for more gravy.

Top: Satay Babi
Bottom: Babi Pong Tay

117 *Pork Ribs In Sweet And Sour Sauce*

PORK RIBS:

A
- 455 g (1 lb) tender pork ribs, cut into 3 cm (1 in) pieces
- Salt water
- $\frac{1}{4}$ teaspoon salt
- $\frac{1}{4}$ teaspoon sugar
- 1 teaspoon monosodium glutamate
- 1 teaspoon ginger juice
- 2 teaspoons light soya sauce
- 1 small egg, beaten with 1 tablespoon cornflour
- 115 g (4 oz) cornflour
- Oil for deep-frying

1. Wash pork ribs in salt water and drain.
2. Mix A in a bowl. Marinate ribs for $\frac{1}{2}$ hour.
3. Roll the marinated ribs in cornflour. Leave to stand for 10 minutes.
4. Deep-fry ribs till cooked. Drain.
5. Arrange on a serving dish to serve with sweet and sour sauce.

SAUCE:

- 1 cucumber

A
- 170 ml (6 fl oz) water
- 1 tablespoon cornflour

B
- $\frac{1}{4}$ teaspoon salt
- $\frac{1}{4}$ teaspoon monosodium glutamate
- 3 tablespoons sugar
- 5 tablespoons tomato ketchup
- 1 teaspoon sesame oil
- 1 teaspoon soya sauce
- 3 tablespoons vinegar
- 2 tablespoons lard

C
- 2 Chinese mushrooms, soaked and shredded
- 1 onion, quartered
- 2 small tomatoes, quartered
- 2 red chillies, seeded and sliced thickly
- 2 stalks spring onions, cut into 5 cm (2 in) lengths

1. Skin the cucumber and cut it lengthwise into quarters. Remove the soft centre and cut into fairly thick pieces, slantwise.
2. Blend A and B in separate bowls.
3. Place lard in a hot pan and stir-fry C for a minute over a high heat. Lower the heat. Add A and B (Step 2) and stir mixture till it boils.
4. Add the cucumber and spring onions. Remove from the heat.
5. Pour sauce over the fried ribs just before serving. Serve hot.

Note:
Green peppers and pineapple can also be added to this dish. Put them in to cook with the other vegetables.

Pork Ribs In Sweet And Sour Sauce

118 *Streaky Pork In Dark Soya Sauce*

A $\left\{\begin{array}{l}\end{array}\right.$
- **1 tablespoon oil**
- **8 cloves garlic, bashed**
- **2 tablespoons sugar**

B $\left\{\begin{array}{l}\end{array}\right.$
- **2–3 tablespoons dark soya sauce**
- **625 g (1 lb 6 oz) streaky pork, cut into pieces**
- **$\frac{3}{4}$ teaspoon salt**
- **$\frac{1}{2}$ teaspoon monosodium glutamate**
- **225 ml (8 fl oz) water**

1. Heat oil in a small saucepan to brown *A*.
2. Add *B*. Stir-fry for 5 minutes. Add one third of the water and cook until the water is absorbed or till the meat is coated with the oily sauce. Stir.
3. Add the rest of the water and boil over a high heat for 5 minutes.
4. Reduce the heat to low, cover saucepan and let simmer till meat is tender, $1-1\frac{1}{4}$ hours. Add more water if necessary, and continue cooking till sauce reaches the consistency required.

Note:
Allow the sugar to turn light brown before adding the meat.

119 *Fillet Steak — Greek-style*

Generous dash of black
pepper
455 g (1 lb) fillet steak, cut
into 1 cm ($\frac{1}{2}$ in) pieces

A {
55 ml (2 fl oz) orange juice
1 tablespoon dark soya sauce
1 heaped tablespoon sugar
1 teaspoon monosodium
glutamate
A pinch of salt
1 teaspoon lemon juice
$\frac{1}{2}$ teaspoon cornflour
1 tablespoon oil

B {
1 piece cinnamon bark, 5 cm
(2 in) in length
2 onions, cut into rings
1 teaspoon sugar
85 g (3 oz) butter

1. Dredge pepper generously on to both sides of steak.
2. Mix *A* in a bowl for the sauce.
3. Heat a heavy-bottomed frying pan. Heat the oil and stir-fry *B* till onions are transparent.
4. Push onions to one side of the pan. Add 55 g butter to melt and brown steak on both sides.
5. Place onions on steak. Add the sauce and stir-fry for $\frac{1}{2}$ minute with the remaining butter.
6. Place steak over onion rings on a serving plate and serve hot.

Note:
Cook steak rare, medium or well done according to taste.

POULTRY

Steamed Stuffed Duck (120)

1·8 kg (3½ lb) duck, whole
    Salt water
    2 tablespoons ginger juice
    2 tablespoons lard or oil

A { 2 slices ginger
    2 cloves garlic, bashed
    4 Chinese mushrooms, soaked in hot water and sliced thinly

225 g (½ lb) pork, chopped coarsely
    Liver and gizzard, diced small

B { ½ teaspoon salt
    1 teaspoon monosodium glutamate
    2 teaspoons light soya sauce
    1 teaspoon brandy
    4 tablespoons pearl barley, soaked in water and drained
    55 g (2 oz) lotus seeds, boiled and drained
    55 g (2 oz) gingko nuts, shelled and skinned

680 ml (24 fl oz) boiling water

1. Wash duck thoroughly with salt water. Wipe dry. Rub ginger juice over the whole duck, including the inside.

2. Heat an iron wok (kuali). Heat lard or oil to stir-fry A till brown. Add the mushrooms and stir-fry for a minute. Add the chopped pork, stir-fry for 2 minutes then add the diced liver and gizzard. Cook for 5 minutes.

3. Remove fried mixture to a saucepan. Add B. Pour in the boiling water and let simmer for ½ hour. Remove the meat mixture and keep gravy aside.

4. Stuff duck with meat mixture. Place duck in a large bowl and pour gravy over. Steam over rapidly boiling water for 3 hours or till duck is tender. Serve hot.

Note:
Add boiling water to the steamer if necessary. Keep the water boiling all the time.

1 big duck, whole
    Salt water

A { 2 tablespoons ginger juice
    8 tablespoons dark soya sauce
    2 tablespoons sugar
    1 tablespoon pepper
    2 teaspoons salt
    1 tablespoon five-spice powder
    1 teaspoon monosodium glutamate
    Lard
    1 tablespoon pounded garlic

B { 5 cm (2 in) piece cinnamon bark
    2 segments star anise
    2 slices galangal

455 ml (16 fl oz) hot water

1. Wash duck thoroughly with salt water. Wipe dry.

2. Mix A in a bowl. Rub 1 tablespoonful of the mixture on to the inside of the duck and 2 tablespoonfuls over the duck. Leave the duck to season for ½ hour.

3. Heat an iron wok (kuali) till very hot. Heat 6 tablespoons lard to brown the duck on all sides over a moderate

122 Diced Chicken With Toasted Almonds

heat, for 10 – 15 minutes, to seal in the juices. Remove the duck to a plate.

4. In a clean pan, heat 3 tablespoons lard or oil. Fry the pounded garlic till light brown and add B.

5. Add the rest of A (Step 2). Pour in the hot water and bring to the boil. Place the duck in and cook over a high heat for 10 minutes. Cover and let duck simmer till tender, about $1-1\frac{1}{4}$ hours. Cool and cut into pieces.

225 g ($\frac{1}{2}$ lb) chicken meat, diced

A
- 1 teaspoon light soya sauce
- 1 teaspoon monosodium glutamate
- $\frac{1}{2}$ teaspoon sugar
- 2 tablespoons oil
- 1 teaspoon cornflour
- 2 tablespoons water

B
- 55 g (2 oz) canned button mushrooms
- 55 g (2 oz) water chestnuts
- 30 g (1 oz) carrots, boiled
- 1 green pepper

115 g (4 oz) almonds, blanched and skinned

4 tablespoons lard or oil

C
- 1 tablespoon light soya sauce
- 1 tablespoon oyster sauce
- 1 teaspoon monosodium glutamate
- 1 teaspoon sesame oil
- 1 teaspoon sugar
- $\frac{1}{4}$ teaspoon pepper
- 1 teaspoon sherry

D
- 1 tablespoon cornflour
- 3 tablespoons water

1. Marinate chicken in A for $\frac{1}{2}$ hour.
2. Dice B.
3. Chop the almonds coarsely. Heat

2 tablespoons lard or oil in an iron wok (kuali) and fry the almonds over a low heat till very light brown. Remove and place on absorbent paper.

4. Increase the heat to high and fry B (Step 2) in the same oil for a minute. Remove to a bowl.

5. Add another 2 tablespoons lard or oil and stir-fry the marinated chicken over a high heat for a minute. Mix C in a bowl and add to chicken together with the fried vegetables. Stir-fry for $\frac{1}{2}$ minute.

6. Blend D and add. Stir and remove to a serving plate.

7. Garnish with the fried almonds. Serve hot.

123 *Chicken In The Basket*

YAM BASKETS [a pair of perforated ladles for making yam baskets is required]:

565 g (20 oz) yam
  4 tablespoons cornflour for
  dusting
  Oil for deep-frying

1. Skin the yam. Do not wash the yam or it will become slimy and difficult to handle. Cut the yam into thin slices. Cut the slices into thin strips, about 0·5 cm broad and 18 cm (7 in) long.

2. Place the yam strips on a tray and dust them with cornflour to keep the strips separated.

3. Put a towel in a bowl. Place a perforated ladle on the towel. Level the yam sticks then spread them, level edge upwards, around the sides of the ladle to form a basket.

4. Fill half a medium-sized saucepan with oil and heat till smoking hot.

5. Press the other ladle lightly over the yam basket and gently dip the sandwiched yam basket into the hot oil to fry for two minutes.

6. Reduce the heat a little to fry till the yam is cooked and turns light brown, about 5–6 minutes. Remove the ladles when the yam basket slips out of the lower ladle. Place on absorbent paper.

7. Make as many baskets as possible, until all the yam strips are used up.

8. Strain the oil to fry the chicken.

Note:
Oil for frying the yam baskets must be sizzling hot. Test it by putting in a strip of yam. If the yam strip sizzles and floats up immediately, the oil is ready for use. Do not wait for the yam to brown in the oil. Fried yam baskets can be stored in an airtight container for 3 weeks.

FILLING:

A {
  1 teaspoon bicarbonate of soda
  1 teaspoon monosodium glutamate
  1 teaspoon sugar
  $\frac{1}{2}$ teaspoon salt
  2 teaspoons light soya sauce
  2 tablespoons cornflour
  3 tablespoons water
  2 tablespoons oil
}

340 g (12 oz) chicken shreds

B {
  3 Chinese mushrooms
  85 g (3 oz) bamboo shoots
  1 large green pepper
  1 large tomato
}

2 tablespoons lard
4 red chillies, seeded and sliced thinly

C {
  1 teaspoon salt
  1 teaspoon monosodium glutamate
  1 teaspoon sugar
  2 teaspoons light soya sauce
  1 teaspoon sesame oil
  1 teaspoon sherry or brandy
  1 tablespoon oyster sauce
  Dash of pepper
}

124 *Seven-minute Crispy Chicken*

D $\left\{\begin{array}{l}\end{array}\right.$
1 tablespoon cornflour
4 tablespoons water
2 stalks spring onions, cut into 5 cm (2 in) lengths
115 g (4 oz) lettuce, shredded

1. Blend *A* in a bowl to marinate the chicken shreds for 1 hour.
2. Heat the strained hot oil in a clean iron wok till smoking hot. Add the seasoned chicken shreds and deep-fry for a minute. Use a perforated ladle to lift chicken shreds on to a plate.
3. Slice *B* thinly into strips.
4. Heat the lard in a clean saucepan. Stir-fry the sliced vegetables and red chillies over a high heat.
5. Reduce the heat and add the fried chicken shreds. Mix *C* in a bowl, add and stir well.
6. Blend *D* in a bowl and add to sauce in pan. Stir well till sauce thickens.
7. Add the spring onions, stir and remove to a dish.

To serve:
Spread shredded lettuce on a large serving plate. Fill baskets with chicken filling and place on top of the lettuce. Serve hot.

0·8 kg (1½–1¾ lb) spring chicken, whole

A $\left\{\begin{array}{l}\end{array}\right.$
2 tablespoons light soya sauce
4 tablespoons water
1 tablespoon sugar
1 tablespoon ginger juice
1 teaspoon sherry
1 teaspoon monosodium glutamate
$\frac{3}{4}$ teaspoon salt
$\frac{1}{2}$ teaspoon cinnamon powder

B $\left\{\begin{array}{l}\end{array}\right.$
115 g (4 oz) self-raising flour
$\frac{1}{4}$ teaspoon salt
$\frac{1}{4}$ teaspoon monosodium glutamate
$\frac{1}{4}$ teaspoon pepper
Oil for deep-frying
1 cucumber, sliced

1. Cut the chicken open from the breast downwards.
2. Turn it over and crack the backbone and thigh bones with the blunt edge of a chopper.
3. Mix *A* in a bowl and marinate the chicken for 1 hour.
4. Sift *B* together to coat the chicken.
5. Heat oil in an aluminium wok (kuali). Deep-fry the chicken for a minute on each side over a high heat. Lower the heat. Fry for another 5 minutes. Turn chicken over once to brown. Lift chicken to drain.
6. Cool for a while before cutting it into pieces. Arrange on a serving dish and garnish with cucumber slices. Serve hot.

125 *Lemon Curried Chicken*

A {
12 shallots
6 candlenuts
4 stalks lemon grass, thinly sliced
1 teaspoon shrimp paste
455 g (16 oz) grated coconut
170 ml (6 fl oz) water

B {
1 tablespoon sugar
1–1½ teaspoons salt
1 teaspoon monosodium glutamate
1 tablespoon curry powder
1·8 kg (4 lb) chicken, cut into pieces
4 tablespoons oil
15–20 pounded dried chillies *or* 4 tablespoons chilli paste
1 stalk lemon grass, bashed lightly

C {
4 tablespoons lemon juice
1 tablespoon tamarind with 115 ml (4 fl oz) water, squeezed and strained
2 lime leaves

1. Grind A to a fine paste.
2. Squeeze grated coconut for No 1 milk. Add water to coconut and squeeze again for the No 2 milk.
3. Mix half of the No 1 milk with B to marinate chicken for ½ hour.
4. Heat an aluminium wok (kuali) till very hot. Heat oil to fry chilli paste over a low heat till oil bubbles through. Add the rest of the No 1 milk, stir-fry for a minute, then add the paste (Step 1) and the lemon grass. Fry till fragrant.
5. Add the marinated chicken and C. Lower the heat and stir-fry till chicken is cooked. Add the No 2 milk and bring to the boil.
6. Reduce the heat to low. Add the lime leaves and let simmer in a covered pan till chicken is tender, ½–¾ hour. Add more water if necessary.

126 *Braised Chicken*

A {
2 tablespoons oil
8 slices ginger
1 tablespoon sugar
3 tablespoons lard

B {
4 tablespoons dark soya sauce
1 tablespoon sugar
½ teaspoon salt
1 teaspoon monosodium glutamate
225 ml (8 fl oz) water

C {
455 g (1 lb) chicken wings
6 chicken livers
6 chicken gizzards
6 chicken legs, cut into two
½ teaspoon sesame oil

1. Heat an iron wok (kuali) till very hot. Heat the oil to fry A. Add 2 tablespoons lard.
2. Pour in B together with half of the water. Add C. Stir and cook for 10 minutes, covered. Remove the livers to a dish. Leave the rest to simmer for ½ hour, covered.
3. Remove the chicken wings to a dish. Pour in the remaining water and let the chicken legs and gizzards continue to simmer till tender. Add the remaining tablespoonful of lard and sesame oil.

To serve:
Slice the cooked livers and gizzards.
Serve hot or cold.

Top: Almond Chicken (127)
Bottom: Spring Chickens (128)

127 Almond Chicken

A {
4 chicken breasts, cut into big pieces
$\frac{1}{2}$ teaspoon salt
1 teaspoon monosodium glutamate
2 teaspoons light soya sauce
2 tablespoons cornflour
1 teaspoon brandy
2 tablespoons water
$\frac{1}{2}$ teaspoon bicarbonate of soda
}

115 g (4 oz) almonds, chopped coarsely
2 tablespoons cornflour
White of an egg
Oil for deep-frying

1. Flatten the chicken.
2. Mix A in a bowl to marinate the chicken for 1 hour.
3. Mix the chopped almonds and the cornflour. Set aside.
4. Beat the egg white till frothy and add the marinated chicken.
5. Coat chicken with the almond mixture and deep-fry in hot oil till light brown. Place chicken on absorbent paper. Serve hot.

128 Spring Chicken

A {
115 g (4 oz) sugar
55 ml (2 fl oz) dark soya sauce
55 ml (2 fl oz) light soya sauce
2 tablespoons wine or sherry
6 cloves
2 tablespoons honey
1 teaspoon monosodium glutamate
1 teaspoon salt
1 teaspoon five-spice powder
2·5 cm (1 in) piece cinnamon bark
570 ml (20 fl oz) water
1 teaspoon sesame oil
}

4 spring chickens, whole, each weighing 455 g (1 lb)
Oil for deep-frying

1. Mix A in a deep saucepan to marinate the chickens for 2 hours.
2. Drain the chickens.
3. Boil the marinade for 10 minutes. Put in the chickens and boil for another 7 minutes.
4. Drain the chickens in a colander till dry.
5. Heat oil in an aluminium wok (kuali) till smoky hot. Put in two chickens. Deep-fry for 2 minutes. Lower the heat a little and fry till golden brown, about 7—10 minutes.
6. Repeat process with the other two chickens.

129 *Paper-wrapped Chicken*

A $\begin{cases}\end{cases}$ Cellophane or 'glass' paper
  - 1 tablespoon cornflour
  - 2 tablespoons water

B $\begin{cases}\end{cases}$
  - 1 teaspoon salt
  - 1 teaspoon monosodium glutamate
  - 1 teaspoon sugar
  - 2 teaspoons sesame oil
  - $\frac{1}{4}$ teaspoon pepper
  - 1 tablespoon light soya sauce
  - 1 tablespoon ginger juice
  - 3 tablespoons lard or oil
  - 1 tablespoon brandy or sherry

1.4 kg (3 lb) chicken, cut into pieces
Oil for deep-frying

1. Cut the cellophane or 'glass' paper into 20 cm (8 in) squares.
2. Blend A in a bowl. Add B, stir well and pour over the chicken. Marinate chicken for 2 hours.
3. Wrap up a few pieces of chicken in each piece of cellophane paper and staple the edges.
4. Heat the oil. Place in the paper-wrapped chicken to fry till light brown. Lift chicken on to a wire sieve to drain.
5. Serve hot in wrappers.

130 *Ayam Kleo*

(Chicken in rich spicy gravy)

A $\begin{cases}\end{cases}$
  - 4 dried chillies
  - 2 red chillies
  - 1 stalk lemon grass, thinly sliced
  - 6 candlenuts
  - 1 thumb-sized piece ginger
  - $\frac{1}{4}$ thumb-sized piece turmeric
  - 3 cloves garlic
  - 15 shallots

1.2 kg (2 $\frac{1}{2}$ lb) chicken, cut into 4 pieces

B $\begin{cases}\end{cases}$
  - 1 teaspoon salt
  - 1 teaspoon monosodium glutamate
  - 2 tablespoons water

625 g (22 oz) grated coconut with 435 ml (14 fl oz) water, squeezed and strained

C $\begin{cases}\end{cases}$
  - 1 teaspoon salt
  - $\frac{1}{2}$ teaspoon monosodium glutamate
  - 1 slice dried tamarind
  - 5 lime leaves
  - 2 stalks lemon grass, lightly bashed

1. Grind A to a fine paste.
2. Marinate the chicken in B and 2 tablespoonfuls of the paste for $\frac{1}{2}$ hour.
3. Pre-heat the grill to hot. Grill the marinated chicken to brown on both sides, about 10 minutes for each side.
4. Mix the rest of the paste with the coconut milk and C, in a saucepan. Put in the chicken and mix well. Cook over a moderate heat for 15 minutes. Reduce the heat and let the chicken simmer till tender. Cook until the gravy is thick and oil comes up to the surface.

137

131 Chicken Stew

A {
- 1·2 kg (2½ lb) chicken, cut into pieces
- 1 tablespoon light soya sauce
- 1 teaspoon monosodium glutamate
- 1 teaspoon sugar
- 1 teaspoon salt
- 1 teaspoon pepper
}

B {
- 10 new potatoes, skinned
- 1 teaspoon peppercorns
- 1 carrot, cut into wedges
- 2 onions, cut into quarters
- 1 chicken cube
- 455 ml (16 fl oz) water
- 2 tablespoons oil
}

C {
- 10 shallots, pounded coarsely
- 1 thumb-sized piece cinnamon bark
- 3 tablespoons butter or margarine
}

D {
- 1 teaspoon dark soya sauce
- 1 teaspoon monosodium glutamate
- ¾ teaspoon salt
- 2 tablespoons flour
- 4 tablespoons water
- 8 tomatoes, cut into halves
}

1. Marinate the chicken in A for ½ hour.
2. Boil B in a saucepan for 10 minutes.
3. Heat the oil in a frying pan and brown C. Remove to a plate.
4. In the same pan, add the butter and fry the marinated chicken to brown on all sides.
5. Mix D in a bowl and add to pan together with B (Step 2) and C (Step 3).
6. Stir and let simmer till chicken is tender, 20 minutes. Add the tomatoes and cook for 5 minutes. Remove from the heat. Serve hot or cold.

132 Ayam Tempra

(Spicy chicken)

A {
- 905 g (2 lb) chicken, cut into pieces
- 1 teaspoon salt
- 1 teaspoon monosodium glutamate
- 8 green chillies
- 6 red chillies
}

B {
- 1 tablespoon dark soya sauce
- 1 tablespoon sugar
- ½ teaspoon monosodium glutamate
- ½ teaspoon salt
- 2 teaspoons lime juice
- 225 ml (8 fl oz) water
- 5 tablespoons oil
- 225 g (8 oz) onions, cut into rings
}

1. Marinate the chicken in A for ½ hour.
2. Slice the chillies slantwise, thickly.
3. Mix B in a bowl.
4. Heat an iron wok (kuali) till very hot. Heat 4 tablespoons oil to fry the onions and chillies for ½ minute.
5. Add the marinated chicken and stir-fry over a high heat till cooked, about 7 minutes. Add B (Step 3) and cook for another 5 minutes.
6. Lower the heat, cover the wok and cook gently for 20 minutes or till

133 *Ayam Sioh*

(Chicken in thick spicy tamarind juice)

the chicken is tender.

7. Remove the lid, add the last tablespoonful of oil, stir well and serve hot or cold.

1·6 kg (3½lb) chicken, quartered
2 tablespoons salt in water
225 g (8 oz) tamarind
340 ml (12 fl oz) water

A
{
3 tablespoons coriander powder, roasted
10 tablespoons sugar
1 tablespoon salt
2 tablespoons dark soya sauce
1 heaped teaspoon pepper
170 g (6 oz) shallots, pounded finely
Oil
}

1. Wash chicken in the salt water. Drain.
2. Soak tamarind in the 340 ml water for 10 minutes. Squeeze and sieve liquid into a deep porcelain bowl.
3. Add *A* and stir well.
4. Add the chicken. Cover and leave to marinate overnight or for at least 10 hours.
5. Transfer the chicken and the marinade to a heavy-bottomed aluminium saucepan and boil for 20 minutes over a moderate heat.
6. Turn the chicken over. Reduce the heat to low and boil for another 20—30 minutes or till chicken is very tender. Remove from heat to

cool before frying chicken pieces in oil Serve hot or cold.

The chicken can also be fried.
1. *Heat an iron wok (kuali) till smoking hot. Add 115 ml oil to heat.*
2. *Put in one or two pieces of chicken to brown on both sides over a low heat.*
3. *Pour some tamarind gravy over the chicken and fry till fragrant and almost dry.*
4. *Place chicken and a little oil on a serving plate.*
5. *Repeat process with the remaining pieces of chicken. Serve hot or cold.*

Note:
Boiled chicken pieces can be kept in the refrigerator for 4—5 days.

134 *Chicken Adoboh*

(Filipino spicy chicken)

A
- 1·6 kg (3½ lb) chicken, cut into pieces
- 2 tablespoons light soya sauce
- 2 – 3 tablespoons vinegar
- 1 tablespoon sugar
- 1 teaspoon pepper
- 1 teaspoon salt
- 4 cloves garlic, chopped coarsely
- 2 tablespoons oil

B
- 285 ml (10 fl oz) water
- 2 chicken cubes
- 4 bay leaves

1. Marinate the chicken in *A* for 1 hour.
2. Boil *B*. Add the chicken and the marinade. Cook for 10 minutes over a high heat, stirring from time to time.
3. Reduce the heat to low and cook till the chicken is tender, about ½ hour, in a covered saucepan.
4. Increase the heat to thicken the gravy just enough to coat the chicken.

Top: Ayam Sioh (133)
Bottom: Chicken In Tomato Curry (135)

135 *Chicken In Tomato Curry*

A
- 115 g (4 oz) shallots
- 2 candlenuts
- 1 stalk lemon grass, sliced
- 4 slices galangal
- 4 slices ginger
- 4 red chillies
- 10 dried chillies
- 10 'chili padi' [optional]
- 1·4 kg (3 lb) chicken, cut into pieces

B
- 1 teaspoon salt
- 1 teaspoon monosodium glutamate
- 1 teaspoon pepper
  Oil
- 2 tablespoons curry powder, mixed into a paste with 3 tablespoons water

C
- 2 tablespoons tomato ketchup
- 4 tomatoes, quartered
- 4 green chillies, slit lengthwise
- 4 red chillies, slit lengthwise
- 2 teaspoons salt
- $\frac{1}{2}$ teaspoon monosodium glutamate
- 2 teaspoons sugar
- 2 tablespoons lime juice

115 g (4 oz) grated coconut with 225 ml (8 fl oz) water, squeezed and strained

1. Grind A till very fine.
2. Marinate the chicken in B for $\frac{1}{2}$ hour. Heat a pan till very hot. Heat enough oil to stir-fry the chicken till brown. Remove to a plate.
3. In a clean hot pan, heat another 4 tablespoons oil. Stir-fry A (Step 1) with the curry paste over a moderate heat till oil bubbles through.
4. Add the fried chicken, C, and half of the coconut milk. Stir for 5 minutes. Pour in the rest of the coconut milk and allow curry to boil. Reduce the heat. Let simmer in covered pan until chicken is tender, about $\frac{1}{2}$ hour.

136 *Enche Kebin*

(Crispy curried chicken)

- 1 chicken, cut into pieces or 905 g (2 lb) chicken wings

A
- 2 tablespoons sugar
- 1 tablespoon evaporated milk
- 1 tablespoon curry powder
- 2 tablespoons ginger juice or 1 teaspoon ginger powder
- 4 teaspoons light soya sauce
- 1 teaspoon pepper
- 1 teaspoon monosodium glutamate
  Oil for deep-frying

B
- 1 cucumber, sliced
- 2 tomatoes, sliced

1. Wash the chicken and wipe dry.
2. Mix A in a bowl to marinate the chicken for 1 hour.
3. Leave the chicken in the sun to dry thoroughly.
4. Heat oil in a pan till smoking hot. Put in the chicken and deep-fry for 2 minutes. Lower the heat and cook till golden brown. Remove to a plate.
5. Garnish with B. Serve hot.

137 *Ayam Buah Keluak*

(Spicy chicken with Indonesian black nuts)

A {
- 1·4 kg (3 lb) chicken, cut into pieces
- 455 g (1 lb) pork ribs, cut into pieces
- 1 teaspoon salt
- 1 teaspoon monosodium glutamate

B {
- 5 candlenuts
- 14 slices galangal
- 2 stalks lemon grass, thinly sliced
- $\frac{1}{2}$ thumb-sized piece turmeric
- 2 tablespoons shrimp paste

C {
- 115 g (4 oz) shallots
- 12 red chillies
- 455 ml (16 fl oz) water
- 3 tablespoons tamarind
- 6 tablespoons oil
- 2 stalks lemon grass, lightly bruised

D {
- 1 teaspoon salt
- 1 teaspoon monosodium glutamate
- 1 teaspoon sugar
- 30 Indonesian black nuts
- 910 ml (32 fl oz) water

1. Marinate the chicken and pork ribs in *A*.
2. Pound *B* till fine. Add *C* and pound coarsely.
3. Add water to the tamarind. Squeeze and strain liquid.
4. Heat an aluminium wok (kuali) till very hot. Add oil to heat and fry paste (Step 2) with the bruised lemon grass till fragrant and brown and oil comes through. Add 2 tablespoonfuls of the tamarind water and stir-fry for a minute. Add *D*, marinated pork ribs and the rest of the tamarind water. Stir and cook over a moderate heat for 20 minutes with lid on.
5. Add the chicken. Stir and add water. Cover and continue cooking till meat is tender, 20 – 25 minutes.

To prepare Indonesian black nuts:
Soak the nuts in water for 5 minutes. Clean the outer shells with a brush. Cut an opening at one end of the nut to remove the 'meat'. Set aside the shells. Pound the 'meat' with $\frac{1}{4}$ teaspoon salt and 1 teaspoon sugar. Return mixture to the empty shells.

Note:
Pound ingredients in the given order.

Butterfly Prawns (147)

SEAFOOD

143

138 *Crab Omelette*

A {
170 g (6 oz) steamed crab meat

2 stalks spring onions, cut into 5 cm (2 in) lengths

1 teaspoon pounded garlic, fried till light brown

115 g (4 oz) boiled streaky pork, shredded thinly

115 g (4 oz) boiled tender bamboo shoots, shredded thinly

1 carrot, skinned and parboiled, shredded thinly

6 eggs, beaten with 3 tablespoons oil and 4 tablespoons water
}

B {
2 tablespoons light soya sauce

1 teaspoon salt

1 teaspoon monosodium glutamate

$\frac{1}{2}$ teaspoon pepper

6 tablespoons lard

2 sprigs Chinese parsley, cut into pieces
}

1. Place *A* in a large bowl. Add *B* and mix well.
2. Heat an iron wok (kuali) till very hot then add 3 tablespoonfuls of the lard to heat. Pour in half of the egg mixture, scramble into bite-sized pieces and remove to a plate. Fry the rest of the omelette mixture with the remainder of the lard.
3. Place the omelette on a serving plate and garnish with parsley. Serve hot or cold.

Crab Omelette

139 Sambal Lengkong

(Crispy fish granules)

A {
340 g (12 oz) shallots
8 candlenuts
3 red chillies, seeded
14 slices galangal, weighing 55 g (2 oz)
6 stalks lemon grass, finely sliced
}

1·2 kg (43 oz) grated coconut
225 ml (8 fl oz) water
1·2 kg (2 lb 11 oz) wolf-herring, washed
2 teaspoons salt
5 tablespoons sugar, mixed with 3 tablespoons hot water
10 lime leaves

1. Pound A to a fine paste.
2. Use a piece of muslin to squeeze the coconut for No 1 milk. Add water to the grated coconut and squeeze for No 2 milk.
3. Place fish in a deep plate. Pour in the No 2 milk and steam over a high heat till fish is cooked. Remove and put aside fish.
4. Mix the fish stock with the No 1 milk and the paste. Add salt.
5. Bone and flake fish very finely. Add to the fish stock and mix well.
6. Heat an iron wok (kuali) till very hot. Pour in the fish mixture to fry over a moderate heat till almost dry, stirring all the time. Reduce the heat to very low and sprinkle the sweetened water. Add the lime leaves and fry until the fish granules are crispy and light brown in colour, stirring constantly. [To test if the fish granules are crispy, press them between thumb and finger. They should be grainy. Cool before storing in an airtight bottle.] Makes 905 g (2 lb) fish granules.

Note:
Steamed fish should be mashed till fine whilst still hot. A mincer may also be used.

140 Crabmeat In Milk Sauce

A {
$\frac{1}{2}$ teaspoon salt
$\frac{1}{2}$ teaspoon monosodium glutamate
$\frac{1}{2}$ teaspoon sugar
1 tablespoon light soya sauce
225 ml (8 fl oz) water
Dash of pepper
}

B {
1 tablespoon cornflour
2 tablespoons water
3 tablespoons lard
}

C {
4 slices ginger
$\frac{1}{4}$ teaspoon pounded garlic
1 egg, beaten with 2 tablespoons water
}

D {
4 tablespoons evaporated milk
1 can white-tipped asparagus
225 g ($\frac{1}{2}$ lb) steamed crab meat
}

1. Mix A and B in separate bowls.
2. Heat 2 tablespoons lard in a hot pan. Fry C till light brown. Pour in A (Step 1) and bring to the boil.
3. Pour in the beaten egg and stir. Add D. Add B (Step 1) and boil for $\frac{1}{2}$ minute. Add the last tablespoonful of lard. Stir mixture in pan and pour into a serving dish. Serve hot.

141 *Ikan Masak Kuah Lada*

(Fish in mild spicy paste)

A {
$\frac{1}{2}$ thumbsized piece turmeric
10 slices galangal
2 stalks lemon grass, sliced
4 candlenuts
1 tablespoon shrimp paste
1 red chilli
12 shallots
1 clove garlic
2 teaspoons pepper
}

3 green egg plants
Salt water
625 g (1 lb 6 oz) Spanish mackerel or ray fish
Sugar and salt for seasoning
5 tablespoons oil
1 walnut-sized tamarind with 225 ml (8 fl oz) water, squeezed and strained

B {
$\frac{1}{2}$ teaspoon salt
$\frac{1}{2}$ teaspoon monosodium glutamate
455 ml (16 fl oz) water
}

1. Grind A to a fine paste.
2. Cut the egg plants into 6 cm ($2\frac{1}{2}$ in) lengths. Halve each piece lengthwise and score the cut surface. Soak in salt water until needed.
3. Wash and cut the fish. Season with 1 teaspoon salt and 1 teaspoon sugar.

Set aside. Heat an aluminium wok (kuali).

4. Heat oil and stir-fry paste (Step 1) over a moderate heat till fragrant. Add the tamarind juice, 2 tablespoonfuls at a time.
5. Add B and boil for 5 minutes. Add the egg plants. Cover wok and cook for 5 minutes. Add the fish and cook till fish is done.

142 *Baked Crabs*

8 medium-sized fresh crabs, whole

A {
1 teaspoon salt
1 teaspoon monosodium glutamate
$\frac{1}{2}$ teaspoon pepper
2 tablespoons lard
1 teaspoon dark soya sauce
1 teaspoon light soya sauce
1 egg, beaten
}

B {
225 g ($\frac{1}{2}$ lb) minced pork, with some fat
225 g ($\frac{1}{2}$ lb) prawns; shelled, de-veined and chopped finely
2 tablespoons breadcrumbs, soaked in 2 tablespoons water
}

Flour for dusting
1 egg, beaten
Breadcrumbs

1. Steam the crabs, whole, over rapidly boiling water for 20 minutes. Cover and do not remove the lid while steaming. Cool. Remove the meat and set aside the shells for the stuffing.
2. Mix A in a bowl.
3. Add B and mix thoroughly. Add the crab meat and mix lightly.

143 *Tempura Prawns*

(Fried prawns — Japanese-style)

4. Dust crab shells with flour. Fill the shells with the crab meat mixture and grill or bake in a pre-heated oven at 190°C (375°F) or Regulo 7 till cooked, about $\frac{1}{2} - \frac{3}{4}$ hour.
5. Remove baked crabs from the oven. Brush with beaten egg and sprinkle on breadcrumbs. Return to the oven for another 5 – 7 minutes. Serve hot or cold.

225 g ($\frac{1}{2}$ lb) small prawns, shelled and deveined
55 g (2 oz) pork chop meat, sliced thinly

A
$\frac{1}{4}$ teaspoon salt
$\frac{1}{2}$ teaspoon brandy
$\frac{1}{2}$ teaspoon monosodium glutamate

B
85 g (3 oz) cauliflower
55 g (2 oz) green peppers

85 g (3 oz) self-raising flour

C
$\frac{1}{2}$ teaspoon salt
$\frac{1}{2}$ teaspoon sugar
$\frac{1}{2}$ teaspoon monosodium glutamate
$\frac{1}{2}$ teaspoon pepper
1 tablespoon oil
130 ml (4$\frac{1}{2}$ fl oz) water
Oil for deep-frying

1. Marinate prawns and pork in *A* for 10 minutes.
2. Slice *B* thinly.
3. Place the flour in a bowl. Stir *C* till well mixed and pour gradually into the flour. Mix well to form a smooth batter. Leave to stand for 20 minutes.
4. Add the marinated prawns, pork and *B*. Stir till well mixed.
5. Heat oil till very hot. Take spoonfuls of the batter and fry till golden brown. Drain on a wire sieve and leave to cool on absorbent paper. Serve hot with sauce.

SAUCE:
4 tablespoons tomato ketchup
1 tablespoon sweet chilli sauce
1 teaspoon 'A 1' brand sauce
1 teaspoon vinegar
1 teaspoon monosodium glutamate
1 teaspoon lime juice
4 tablespoons boiled water, cooled

1. Mix all the ingredients in a bowl.
2. Serve in a separate bowl with the fried prawns.

147

144 Sambal Tempe

(Spicy fermented soya beans)

A {
10 shallots
10 cloves garlic
6 red chillies
10 green chillies
2 stalks lemon grass
}

225 g (8 oz) grated coconut
225 ml (8 fl oz) water
   Oil
2 soya bean cakes, diced small
1 teaspoon dried chilli paste
   or 10 – 15 dried chillies

B {
1 teaspoon salt
2 teaspoons sugar
1 teaspoon monosodium
   glutamate
2 packets fermented soya
   beans, diced
2 slices galangal
20 quail's eggs, hard-boiled
   and shelled
2 stalks lemon grass, bruised
}

455 g (1 lb) small prawns,
   shelled and deveined

1. Slice A finely.
2. Fry the sliced ingredients separately till light brown.
3. Use muslin to squeeze coconut for No 1 milk. Set aside. Add water to coconut and squeeze for No 2 milk.
4. Heat an iron wok (kuali) till very hot. Heat oil to fry diced soya bean cakes for 2 minutes. Remove to a plate.
5. Leave 2 tablespoons oil in wok and stir-fry chilli paste and 2 tablespoons No 1 milk for a minute.
6. Add the No 2 milk, fried ingredients and B.
7. Stir and cook over a low heat for 5 minutes. Add prawns. Cover pan and cook for 2 minutes. Stir-fry and remove to a serving dish. Serve hot or cold.

145 Sambal Udang

(Spicy prawns)

A {
15 shallots
30 dried chillies or 3 tablespoons chilli paste
1 tablespoon shrimp paste
1 clove garlic
}

6 tablespoons oil
115 g (4 oz) grated coconut with
   55 ml (2 fl oz) water for
   milk

B {
905 g (2 lb) small prawns,
   shelled
1 teaspoon sugar
½ teaspoon salt
   Pinch of monosodium
   glutamate
1 tablespoon tamarind with
   55 ml (2 fl oz) water,
   squeezed and strained
}

1. Grind A to a paste.
2. Heat an aluminium wok (kuali). Heat oil and fry paste over a moderate heat till oil bubbles through.
3. Add half of the coconut milk and stir for 2 minutes. Add B. Cover and cook for another 2 minutes. Add the rest of the coconut milk. Stir for a minute and serve.

146 Fried Chillied Cuttlefish

A {
  15 red chillies
  $\frac{1}{2}$ teaspoon shrimp paste

  455 g (1 lb) cuttlefish
  6 tablespoons lard or oil
  2 big onions, sliced thinly

B {
  $\frac{1}{2}$ teaspoon salt
  1 teaspoon sugar
  $\frac{1}{2}$ teaspoon monosodium glutamate
  1 teaspoon lime juice

1. Pound A to a fine paste.
2. Remove ink bag and bone from cuttlefish. Wash, drain and cut cuttlefish into 2·5 cm (1 in) rings.
3. Heat an iron wok (kuali) till very hot. Heat 3 tablespoons lard. Fry cuttlefish over a high heat for 5 minutes. Remove to a dish.
4. Heat the rest of the lard and fry the sliced onions over a high heat for a minute. Reduce the heat, add the paste and B and stir-fry for another minute. Add the cuttlefish and stir well with the paste. Serve hot or cold.

Note:
Cuttlefish comes in 2 sizes, the small cuttlefish and the larger, longish type. For this dish, the longish type is more suitable.

Fried Chillied Cuttlefish

A
{
  1 egg, lightly beaten
  1 tablespoon cornflour
  1 tablespoon water
  A pinch of salt
  Dash of pepper
}
455 g (1 lb) big prawns
'Paxo' brand golden crumbs
Oil for deep-frying
Sliced cucumber and
tomatoes

1. Mix *A* in a bowl.
2. Remove the head and shell from each prawn, but leave the tail and last segment unshelled. Slice the prawn lengthwise without cutting through. Remove the dark vein.
3. Spread prawn open, and flatten the thick part of each prawn with the back of a chopper. Make a small slit in the centre of the flattened prawn. Push the tail through the slit so that the prawn resembles a butterfly.
4. Place the prawns spread open on a large plate. Leaving the tail end clean, coat each prawn well with *A*.
5. Spread the crumbs on a plate and coat prawns with golden crumbs. [Remember to leave the tail end free of crumbs.]
6. Deep-fry prawns in hot oil over a moderate heat for a minute. Remove and serve with sliced cucumber and tomatoes. Serve hot.

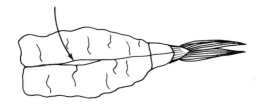

Note:
Do not overfry or crumbs will be discoloured.

1. *Slice lengthwise, without cutting through.*

2. *Make a small slit through the centre of each flattened prawn.*

3. *Push the tail through the slit so that the prawn resembles a butterfly.*

148 Steamed Pomfret

A
{
2 teaspoons light soya sauce
1 teaspoon monosodium
glutamate
$\frac{1}{2}$ teaspoon sugar
$\frac{1}{2}$ teaspoon sesame oil
$\frac{1}{4}$ teaspoon fine salt
225 ml (8 fl oz) chicken stock
}

2 dried mushrooms, soaked
in hot water
1 pomfret, 455 – 680 g
(1–1$\frac{1}{2}$ lb)
Salt
10 thin slices ginger
2 tablespoons lard
1 tablespoon pork fat, finely
shredded

B
{
1 tablespoon cooked ham,
finely shredded
1 stalk Chinese parsley, cut
2 red chillies, cut into strips
2 stalks spring onions, cut into
5 cm (2 in) lengths
}

1. Mix A in a bowl for the sauce.
2. Slice the mushrooms into strips.
3. Clean the fish and make two shallow slits on each side. Season with salt.
4. Arrange half of the ginger slices and spread 1 tablespoonful of the lard on a plate. Place the fish on top.
5. Spread the rest of the ginger, pork fat and mushroom strips over the fish.
6. Steam for 12 – 15 minutes over a very high heat or till cooked.
7. Boil the sauce in another pan. Stir in the other tablespoonful of lard.
8. Place the steamed fish on a hot serving dish and pour the cooked sauce over the fish. Garnish with B and serve while very hot.

149 Ikan Terobok Goreng

(Fish in screw pine leaves)

905 g (2 lb) herring, whole or cut
into two pieces
1 teaspoon salt
6 screw pine leaves
225 ml (8 fl oz) oil

1. Wash the fish, rub it with the salt and leave to marinate for $\frac{1}{2}$ hour.
2. Wrap the screw pine leaves round the fish.
3. Heat an iron wok (kuali). Heat the oil. Place the fish in wok and cover. Fry till fish is cooked, crisp and brown on both sides.
4. Remove the screw pine leaves and place the fish on a plate. Pour the hot oil over it and serve hot.

Note:
Do not scale the fish. The fish should be fried over a moderately high heat so that it is thoroughly cooked and the scales are crisp. Sprinkle some water whilst frying before covering the pan. The steam from the water will hasten the cooking.

455 g (1 lb) fish slices [thread-
fin or grouper]

A {
$\frac{3}{4}$ teaspoon salt
1 teaspoon monosodium
glutamate
1 teaspoon sugar
$\frac{1}{4}$ teaspoon pepper
1 tablespoon light soya sauce
1 tablespoon ginger juice
1 tablespoon cornflour
Self-raising flour
Oil for deep-frying
}

B {
1 tablespoon light soya sauce
3 tablespoons sugar
$\frac{1}{2}$ teaspoon monosodium
glutamate
4 tablespoons tomato
ketchup
1 teaspoon sweet chilli sauce
1–2 tablespoons vinegar
1 teaspoon dark soya sauce
1 tablespoon 'HP' sauce
3 tablespoons lard
}

C {
4 slices ginger
1 onion, sliced
2 tomatoes, quartered
3 dried mushrooms, soaked
and sliced
}

D {
2 tablespoons cornflour
170 ml (6 fl oz) water
}

E {
1 cucumber, without centre;
cut into thick strips,
slantwise
2 stalks spring onions, cut
into 5 cm (2 in) lengths
2 red chillies, cut into thin
long strips and soaked in
iced water
}

1. Marinate the fish in *A* for $\frac{1}{2}$ hour.
2. Drain and coat with self-raising
flour on both sides.
3. Heat oil in pan till very hot. Put
in the fish and fry until light brown.
Remove to a deep serving plate.
4. Mix *B* in a bowl for the sauce. Set
aside.
5. Heat 2 tablespoons lard in a hot pan.
6. Over a very high heat, stir-fry *C* for a
minute. Blend *D* in a bowl and pour
into the pan. Add the sauce.
7. Bring to the boil, add the cucumber
strips and cook for $\frac{1}{2}$ minute. Add
the last tablespoonful of lard. Remove
and pour sauce into a sauceboat.
8. Pour the sauce over the fish just before serving and garnish with *E*.

Note:
*To ensure that fish is crispy, re-fry fish in hot
oil just before serving. Serve hot.*

A {
10 shallots
6 dried chillies *or* 1 tablespoon
chilli paste
1 teaspoon shrimp paste
1 candlenut
1 stalk lemon grass, sliced
}
310 g (11 oz) shelled cockles
5 tablespoons oil
1 stalk lemon grass, bruised

B {
115 ml (4 fl oz) water
1 teaspoon tamarind with
115 ml (4 fl oz) water,
squeezed and strained
1 teaspoon sugar
1 teaspoon salt
$\frac{1}{2}$ teaspoon monosodium
glutamate
}
115 g (4 oz) grated coconut,
squeezed with 115 ml (4 fl
oz) water for milk

1. Pound *A* to a fine paste.
2. Scald the cockles and drain in a
colander.
3. Heat a pan till very hot. Heat the oil.
Fry the paste and bruised lemon
grass till fragrant.
4. Add *B*. Allow mixture to boil.
5. Add the cockles and coconut milk.

Ikan Masak Pedas

(Fish in mild spicy tamarind juice)

6. Cook for a minute and remove to a dish.

625 g (22 oz) silver belly or grouper

A {
14 slices galangal
$\frac{1}{2}$ thumb-sized piece turmeric
1 candlenut
1 heaped tablespoon shrimp paste
}

B {
20 shallots
5 red chillies
}

C {
680 ml (24 fl oz) water
$1\frac{1}{2}$ walnut-sized tamarind with 225 ml (8 fl oz) water, squeezed and strained
3 dried tamarind slices
$\frac{1}{2}$ tablespoon salt
1 teaspoon sugar
}

D {
4 sprigs basil leaves, picked and washed
1 tablespoon lard
}

1. Clean the fish and sprinkle some salt over it.
2. Pound A in the given order to a fine paste. Add B and continue to pound coarsely.
3. Mix the paste and C in an enamel saucepan and boil for 15 minutes.
4. Add the fish. Reduce the heat and let simmer, uncovered, till fish is cooked, 5 – 7 minutes.
5. Garnish with D. Serve hot, with chillied shrimp paste (page 187).

153 Udang Kuah Pedas Nenas

(Prawns in pineapple gravy)

A {
- 14 slices galangal
- $\frac{1}{2}$ thumb-sized piece turmeric
- 1 candlenut
- 3 red chillies
- 1 tablespoon shrimp paste

B {
- 910 ml (32 fl oz) water
- 1 tablespoon salt
- 1 tablespoon sugar
- 1 pineapple, cut into thin pieces
- 2 dried tamarind slices

- 625 g (1 lb 6 oz) king prawns, washed and trimmed
- Sprigs of basil leaves

1. Pound A in the given order to a fine paste.
2. Transfer the paste to an enamel saucepan. Add B and mix well. Boil over a moderate heat for 10 minutes.
3. Add the prawns, cook uncovered for 2 minutes. Remove from the heat. Garnish with basil leaves. Serve hot.

Note:
The gravy can be boiled first. Add the prawns to cook just before serving so that the prawns will be sweet and more tasty.

154 Prawns With Cashew Nuts

- 455 g (1 lb) medium-sized prawns, shelled and de-veined

A {
- $\frac{1}{4}$ teaspoon salt
- 1 teaspoon sugar
- $\frac{1}{4}$ teaspoon monosodium glutamate
- Dash of pepper
- $\frac{1}{2}$ teaspoon ginger juice
- 1 tablespoon cornflour
- 1 teaspoon oil

B {
- $\frac{1}{4}$ teaspoon salt
- $\frac{1}{4}$ teaspoon monosodium glutamate
- $\frac{1}{4}$ teaspoon sugar
- 1 teaspoon light soya sauce
- 1 teaspoon cornflour
- 6 tablespoons water
- 1 teaspoon sherry
- Oil for deep-frying

C {
- 115 g (4 oz) roasted or fried cashew nuts
- 1 stalk spring onions, cut into 5 cm (2 in) lengths
- 1 tablespoon lard

1. Marinate prawns in A for $\frac{1}{2}$ –1 hour.
2. Mix B in a bowl for the sauce.
3. Heat oil for deep-frying till very hot. Put in the marinated prawns and cook for a minute. Remove and drain.
4. Leave only about 2 tablespoons oil in the pan. Pour in the sauce and stir well. Add C and the cooked prawns. Dish on to a serving plate and serve immediately.

Note:
Soak the shelled prawns in iced water for 1 hour with a teaspoon of sugar before marinating to make them crunchy.

155 Assam Gulai

(Fish in spicy tamarind juice)

A {
310 g (11 oz) lady's fingers
2 dried tamarind slices
1 tablespoon sugar
A pinch of salt
Water

B {
3 stalks lemon grass, thinly sliced
$\frac{1}{2}$ thumb-sized piece turmeric
20 dried chillies or 2–3 table-spoons chilli paste
20 shallots
2 cloves garlic
1 tablespoon shrimp paste

115 ml (4 fl oz) oil

C {
2 tablespoons sugar
2 teaspoons salt
$\frac{1}{2}$ teaspoon monosodium glutamate
2 stalks phaeomaria (bunga kantan) , halved lengthwise

1 –1$\frac{1}{2}$ tablespoons tamarind with 910 ml (32 fl oz) water, squeezed and strained
625 g (1 lb 6 oz) prawns or fish head, trimmed and washed

1. Cut away the stems of the lady's fingers before halving them.
2. Boil A in a saucepan. Put in the lady's fingers and boil till tender, 10 – 15 minutes. Drain and set aside.
3. Grind B to a fine paste.
4. Heat an aluminium wok (kuali). Heat the oil to fry the paste till oil bubbles through, stirring constantly.
5. Stir in C and some of the tamarind water.
6. Cook for a minute, then add the rest of the tamarind water and bring to the boil. Do not cover wok.
7. Boil for 2 minutes. Put in the prawns or fish head and cook till done. Finally, add the lady's fingers.

Note:
To choose young and tender lady's fingers, bend the ends to see if they snap easily. Those that do not break easily are tough and stringy.

156 Prawns In Soya Sauce

A {
4 tablespoons light soya sauce
1 tablespoon sugar
1 teaspoon cornflour
2 tablespoons water

455 g (1 lb) prawns, fairly large
Salt water
8 tablespoons lard or oil
2 thumb-sized pieces ginger, shredded finely
$\frac{1}{4}$ teaspoon salt
2 stalks spring onions, cut into short lengths

1. Mix A in a bowl for the sauce.
2. Trim off the prawn whiskers and wash the prawns in salt water. Drain.
3. Heat the lard in an iron wok (kuali) till very hot. Fry the ginger till brown. Add the prawns, salt and stir-fry for $\frac{1}{2}$ minute. Cover and cook for 5 – 7 minutes or till prawns are cooked.
4. Remove the lid, add the sauce, stir well with the prawns and add the spring onions. Serve.

157 Tomato Chillied Crabs

A {
- 1 tablespoon chilli sauce
- 2 tablespoons light soya sauce
- $\frac{1}{4}$ teaspoon salt
- 1 tablespoon sugar
- $\frac{1}{2}$ teaspoon monosodium glutamate
- 2 tablespoons vinegar
- 8 tablespoons tomato ketchup
- 1 teaspoon sesame oil
- 340 ml (12 fl oz) water
}

B {
- 4 cloves garlic
- 10 shallots
- $\frac{1}{2}$ thumb-sized piece ginger
}

C {
- 2 tablespoons cornflour
- 4 tablespoons water
}

- 6 tablespoons lard
- 1·5 kg (3 $\frac{1}{4}$ lb) crabs, cleaned and cut into pieces
- 1 egg, beaten

1. Mix A in a bowl for the sauce.
2. Pound B to a fine paste.
3. Blend C in a separate bowl for the thickening.
4. Heat an iron wok (kuali). Heat 4 tablespoons lard to fry the paste till fragrant. Add the crabs and one-third of the sauce. Stir-fry for 2 minutes over a high heat.
5. Add the rest of the sauce; stir and cover wok for 10 minutes. [Do not remove the lid before the 10 minutes.]
6. Add the thickening and stir well. Add the beaten egg, mix thoroughly with the chillied crabs and remove to a serving plate. Serve at once.

158 Fish Head Curry

- 6 red chillies
- 8 green chillies
- 5 tablespoons oil
- 1 tablespoon mixed curry seeds for fish curry*
- $\frac{1}{2}$ thumb-sized piece ginger, thinly shredded
- 2 cloves garlic, sliced thinly
- 2 onions, sliced thinly
- 4 tablespoons curry powder, mixed into a paste with 225 ml (8 fl oz) water
- 225 g (8 oz) grated coconut, squeezed with 225 ml (8 fl oz) water

A {
- 1 – 2 teaspoons salt
- 2 – 3 teaspoons sugar
- 1 teaspoon monosodium glutamate
- 3 tomatoes, quartered
- 55 g (2 oz) tamarind with 225 ml (8 fl oz) water, squeezed and strained
- 2 sprigs curry leaves
}

- 225 g (8 oz) tender lady's fingers
- 625 g (1 lb 6 oz) fish head

1. Slit the chillies half-way, lengthwise.
2. Heat an aluminium wok (kuali). Heat the oil and fry the curry

seeds and ginger till light brown. Add the garlic and stir-fry for $\frac{1}{2}$ minute. Add the sliced onion and fry till soft and transparent. Add the curry paste and 115 ml of the coconut milk. Stir-fry till the oil comes through.

3. Add A and continue to cook over a low heat. Add the remaining coconut milk. Let simmer for 5 minutes.

4. Add sliced chillies and the fish head, cover pan and let simmer till cooked.

*See "Helpful Hints".

Note:
You can add 3—4 dried tamarind slices for a sharp, sourish taste.

Fish Head Curry

159 Sambal Udang Kering Goreng

(Fried dried prawns)

A {
  6 candlenuts
  1 thumb-sized piece turmeric
  1 teaspoon shrimp paste

B {
  6 tablespoons sugar
  $\frac{1}{2}$ tablespoon salt
  3 tablespoons tamarind with
    140 ml (5 fl oz) water,
    squeezed and strained
  340 g (12 oz) dried prawns,
    soaked and pounded till fine

C {
  115 g (4 oz) green chillies
  115 g (4 oz) red chillies
  115 g (4 oz) garlic
  225 g (8 oz) shallots
  10 stalks lemon grass

285 ml (10 fl oz) oil

1. Pound A to a paste. Add B and mix thoroughly.
2. Slice C finely. [The lemon grass should be sliced slantwise.]
3. Heat an iron wok (kuali). Heat the oil. Fry the sliced ingredients separately till light brown. Remove.
4. Leave the oil in the wok and fry the dried prawn mixture over a low heat till almost dry. Add all the fried ingredients.
5. Stir-fry for 5 minutes and remove to a tray to cool.

Note:
Stir the dried prawn mixture constantly when cooking, to prevent it from burning. This dish can be kept for months if stored in a refrigerator. When using an electric blender, do not soak or wash the dried prawns. Blend a little at a time.

160 Ikan Masak Assam Pekat

(Fish in thick tamarind juice)

A {
  1 thumb-sized piece turmeric
  2 tablespoons shrimp paste
  8 shallots

6 green chillies
6 red chillies
625 g (22 oz) Spanish mackerel, cut into 2·5 cm (1 in) cubes
170 g (6 oz) tamarind with
  425 ml (15 fl oz) water,
  squeezed and strained

B {
  6 tablespoons sugar
  $1\frac{1}{2}$ teaspoons salt
  1 teaspoon lard or oil

1. Grind A to a fine paste.
2. Slit the chillies lengthwise.
3. Wash and marinate the fish in a little salt and tamarind water for $\frac{1}{2}$ hour.
4. Boil the tamarind water, the paste, and B in an enamel saucepan. Boil gently for 15 minutes. Put in the fish to cook.
5. Add the chillies and continue cooking for another minute. Lastly, mix in the lard. Serve hot or cold.

161 Chillied King Prawns

A {
15 **red chillies**
1 **teaspoon shrimp paste**
$\frac{1}{4}$ **teaspoon salt**
6 **tablespoons oil**

625 g (22 oz) **king prawns, trimmed**
$\frac{1}{2}$ **teaspoon salt**
1 **big onion sliced**

B {
1 **teaspoon sugar**
1 **tablespoon lime juice**

1. Pound *A* till fine.
2. Heat an iron wok (kuali). Heat the oil. Fry the prawns till cooked. Add salt and sliced onions.
3. Push to one side of the wok and fry the chilli paste (Step 1). Stir in the prawns and onions, season with *B*, and fry for a minute. Remove to a serving plate.

Chillied King Prawns

RICE AND NOODLES

162 *Nasi Lemak*

(Coconut milk rice)

680 g (24 oz) No 1 Thai rice
625 g (22 oz) grated coconut, white
455 ml (16 fl oz) water
1$\frac{1}{2}$ teaspoons salt
6 screw pine leaves, tied into a knot

1. Wash the rice and soak it in water for 2 hours. Drain before use.
2. Use a piece of muslin to squeeze 225 ml (8 fl oz) No 1 milk from the grated coconut.
3. Add the 455 ml water and squeeze for No 2 milk. Measure, then add water to obtain 740 ml (26 fl oz) No 2 milk.
4. Put the rice in the rice cooker, stir in the No 2 milk and the salt. Boil till rice is dry. Place the screw pine leaves on top and leave rice in the cooker for a further $\frac{1}{2}$ hour.
5. Rake the rice with a fork, add the No 1 milk and stir lightly to mix.
6. Leave the rice in the cooker to absorb the milk for another 20 minutes. Serve hot or cold.

Note:
Stir rice once or twice whilst boiling. Do not stir any more when the rice is dry. Stir again only when adding the No 1 milk. Use an electric rice cooker.

[10 servings]

163 *Chicken Congee*

雞粥

A {
  225 g (8 oz) rice
  2 tablespoons glutinous rice, optional

B {
  2 teaspoons salt
  1 tablespoon oil

2·3 litres (80 fl oz) water

C {
  905 g (2 lb) chicken, whole, cleaned
  1 teaspoon pepper
  1 teaspoon salt

D {
  1 teaspoon sesame oil
  1 teaspoon monosodium glutamate
  1 tablespoon light soya sauce

910 ml (32 fl oz) water
1 chicken cube

E {
  1 teaspoon monosodium glutamate
  1–2 tablespoons salt or to taste

F {
  4 stalks spring onions, cut into small pieces
  1½ thumb-sized piece tender ginger, shredded thinly
  2 crispy Chinese crullers, sliced

1. Wash *A* till the water runs clear. Drain and place in a bowl. Add *B*, mix well and set aside.
2. Boil the 2·3 litres water in a deep pan.

Put in *C* and boil rapidly for 5 minutes. Cover the pan and let simmer for 45 minutes.

3. Remove the chicken and immerse it in a basin of cold water for 10 minutes. Bone the chicken and return the bones to the stock to boil gently for 1 hour.
4. Dice the chicken meat, put in a bowl and season with *D*. Mix well and set aside.
5. Boil the 910 ml water in a deep saucepan. Add the rice and boil rapidly for 10 minutes.
6. Pour in the chicken stock, add the chicken cube and continue boiling over a moderate heat for 1 hour or till congee is thick and smooth, stirring occasionally.
7. Stir in *E*. Let simmer till ready to serve, stirring occasionally. Add some boiling water if congee is too thick. Stir well.

To serve chicken congee:

1. Serve congee in small individual bowls.
2. Add some chicken meat and garnish with *F*.
3. Add a dash of pepper and serve hot.

Note:
Transparent bean vermicelli, fried to a crisp, can be used instead of the crispy Chinese crullers.
1. *Heat oil for deep-frying till smoking hot. Put in about 15 g dry transparent bean vermicelli. Submerge vermicelli with a Chinese frying slice and fry till it turns crisp and white.*
2. *Remove immediately from the oil.*
3. *Cool and store in an airtight container till ready to serve.*

164 *Nasi Pilau*

(Buttered rice with roast chicken)

A {
1 teaspoon salt
1 teaspoon monosodium glutamate
1 teaspoon pepper
1 teaspoon brandy
1 teaspoon sugar
1 tablespoon ginger juice
1 tablespoon light soya sauce
}

1·4 kg (3 lb) chicken, whole
170 g (6 oz) butter
115 ml (4 fl oz) water

B {
625 g (22 oz) No 1 Thai rice
1 litre (36 fl oz) water
}

1 handful raisins, fried
30 almonds, sliced and fried
6 slices cooked ham, cut into pieces and rolled
A few lettuce leaves
1 cucumber, sliced

1. Mix A in a bowl for the seasoning.
2. Marinate the inside of the chicken using 1 tablespoonful of the seasoning. Then marinate the outside of the chicken. Leave for an hour.
3. Heat the oven till very hot. Heat the roasting pan. Grease chicken with half of the butter. Place it in the heated pan. Add water to the leftover marinade, mix well and pour into the roasting pan. Roast chicken for $\frac{1}{2}$ hour till brown. Reduce the heat to moderate and continue roasting till the chicken is cooked, $\frac{3}{4}$ – 1 hour.
4. Bone and cut the chicken into serving portions. Set aside. Leave the juices in the pan.
5. Cook B in a rice cooker.
6. Rake rice with a fork, add the rest of the butter, pan juices and mix well.
7. Dish the rice on to a large serving plate. Scatter the raisins and almonds. Arrange the chicken and rolled ham on top. Garnish the border of the dish with lettuce and cucumber.

[10 servings]

165 *Fried Noodles*

910 ml (32 fl oz) water

A {
1 packet dried egg noodles
1 chicken cube
1 tablespoon lard
Oil or lard
}

6 eggs, lightly beaten with a pinch of salt
2 tablespoons lard
1 teaspoon pounded garlic
115 g ($\frac{1}{4}$ lb) small, cooked prawns, shelled
455 g (16 oz) bean sprouts, washed and picked
225 g ($\frac{1}{2}$ lb) roast pork, shredded finely

B {
1 tablespoon oyster sauce
$\frac{1}{2}$ teaspoon salt
2 tablespoons light soya sauce
1 teaspoon sesame oil
$\frac{1}{2}$ teaspoon pepper
1 teaspoon monosodium glutamate
$\frac{1}{2}$ teaspoon sugar
115 ml (4 fl oz) hot water
}

C {
225 g (8 oz) lettuce, cut into strips
2 – 3 chillies, seeded and cut into long thin strips
}

166 *Nasi Lontong*

(Compressed rice cakes)

1. Boil the water in a saucepan. Add *A*. Boil for 5–7 minutes or till noodles separate. Immerse in cold water. Drain in a colander.
2. Heat an iron wok (kuali) till very hot. Heat the oil and scramble the eggs. Remove to a dish.
3. In the same wok, add 2 tablespoons lard. Fry the garlic till light brown. Add the prawns and stir-fry for $\frac{1}{2}$ minute.
4. Add the bean sprouts, noodles, eggs and roast pork.
5. Toss mixture in the wok. Mix *B* in a bowl and pour over and around the noodle mixture. Stir-fry and cook for 2 minutes.
6. Remove noodles to a large serving plate. Garnish with *C* and serve.

625 g (22 oz) No 1 Thai rice
1·2 litres (42 fl oz) water
$\frac{1}{2}$ teaspoon salt
6 screw pine leaves, tied into a knot

1. Wash and soak the rice overnight. Drain before use.
2. Wet two 10 cm x 20 cm (4 in x 8 in) cloth bags and fill each with half the rice. Stitch to seal the open end.
3. Boil the water in a heavy-bottomed aluminium saucepan. Add salt and screw pine leaves.
4. Place the cloth bags in the saucepan. The water should be 8 cm (3 in) above the bags. Add boiling water when necessary. Boil for 2 hours and remove.
5. Wrap the bags with a dry towel and place a bread board and a weight on top. Leave until the rice is firm and cold, at least 8 – 10 hours.
6. Unstitch the bags to remove the rice. Cut it into long strips with a wet knife and cut again into thin squares, using a thick white thread.

[10 servings]

Note:
It is best to cook the rice in the evening and leave it pressed overnight.
Place an enamel plate in the saucepan before putting in the bag of rice to prevent it from sticking to the pan.

905 g (2 lb) boned chicken, cut into pieces

A
- 1 teaspoon salt
- 1 teaspoon monosodium glutamate
- 1 teaspoon dark soya sauce
- 2 tablespoons oil

115 ml (4 fl oz) lard or oil

B
- 1 thumb-sized piece ginger, shredded finely
- 3 cloves garlic, thinly sliced
- 4 shallots, thinly sliced
- 4 dried Chinese mushrooms, soaked and sliced thinly

625 g (22 oz) No 1 Thai rice, washed and drained

C
- 2 tablespoons light soya sauce
- 1 teaspoon dark soya sauce
- 1 teaspoon monosodium glutamate
- 1 teaspoon salt
- 1 tablespoon sesame oil
- 1 chicken cube, mashed
- $\frac{1}{4}$ teaspoon pepper

935 ml (33 fl oz) boiling water

2 pairs Chinese sausages, fried and cut into 4 cm ($1\frac{1}{2}$ in) pieces

Chinese parsley

1. Marinate the chicken in A for $\frac{1}{2}$ hour.
2. Heat a pan till very hot. Heat the 2 tablespoons oil to fry the chicken till brown on all sides. Set aside in a dish.
3. Heat lard in an iron wok (kuali) and fry B till light brown. Add the mushrooms and stir-fry for a minute. Add the rice and fry till the oil is absorbed.
4. Remove the rice to a saucepan or an electric rice cooker. Mix C in a bowl and add to the rice together with the boiling water. Cook till the rice is quite dry.
5. Place the fried sausages and the fried chicken pieces on the rice. Allow to cook for $\frac{1}{2}$ hour over a low heat. Serve hot.

To serve:
Rake rice with a fork. Spoon rice on to a large serving plate. Arrange the chicken and sausages on top of rice. Garnish with Chinese parsley.

Note:
Wipe the water from under the lid of the rice cooker whilst cooking to prevent the rice from becoming soggy.

[8–10 servings]

Opposite page
Left: Fried Noodles (165)
Right: Flavoured Chicken Rice

4 tablespoons lard or oil

4 eggs, lightly beaten with a pinch of salt

2 tablespoons chopped onions

85 g (3 oz) small shelled prawns

455 g (16 oz) cold cooked rice

A
- 6 tablespoons water
- 1 teaspoon salt
- 1 teaspoon monosodium glutamate
- 1 tablespoon light soya sauce
- $\frac{1}{4}$ teaspoon pepper

115 g ($\frac{1}{4}$ lb) roast pork, diced

4 tablespoons chopped spring onions

1. Heat an iron wok (kuali) till very hot. Heat 2 tablespoons lard and scramble the beaten eggs. Remove and set aside.
2. Heat the rest of the lard and fry the onions till transparent. Add the prawns and stir-fry.
3. Add the rice and stir-fry. Mix A in a bowl and add to the rice, stir-frying all the time.
4. Add the scrambled eggs and roast pork. Continue to stir-fry over a high heat. Finally add the spring onions. Serve fried rice hot in a large dish.

Fried Rice

169 *Hokien Fried Noodles*

福建炸麵

A {
310 g (11 oz) medium prawns
1 tablespoon oil
225 ml (8 fl oz) water
455 ml (16 fl oz) water
1 teaspoon salt
2 teaspoons monosodium
glutamate
310 g (11 oz) cuttlefish [remove the centre bone and ink bag]
310 g (11 oz) streaky pork
Lard for frying

B {
4 eggs
625 g (22 oz) bean sprouts, picked and washed
625 g (22 oz) fresh yellow noodles
2 teaspoons pounded garlic
2 tablespoons light soya sauce
55 g (2 oz) chives, cut into 3 cm lengths

C {
4 limes, halved
4 red chillies, sliced thinly

To make the stock:

1. Remove the prawn heads. Wash and drain them. Fry the heads in 1 tablespoon oil for a minute. Remove from the pan and pound. Mix with the 225 ml water. Strain and set liquid aside.

2. Boil A in a saucepan.

3. Put in the cuttlefish to boil for 2 minutes. Remove and cut into thin rounds. Set aside.

4. Cook the prawns in the same stock. Remove and shell but leave the tail on. Set aside.

5. Put the streaky pork in the stock and boil till done, about 15 minutes. Set aside to cool. Slice the pork into thin pieces, then cut into thin strips. Set aside.

6. Pour the prawn liquid (Step 1) into the stock and continue boiling till the stock is reduced to 455 ml (16 fl oz). Strain.

To fry the noodles:

1. Halve B and the cooked prawns, pork and cuttlefish to fry in two separate lots.

2. Heat a large iron wok (kuali) till very hot. Heat 2 tablespoons lard to fry one lot. Break in the eggs and spread thinly to cook in the wok. Add the bean sprouts and noodles. Add 1 tablespoonful (85 ml or 3 fl oz) of the stock to the noodles, stir-fry and cover. Cook for a moment.

3. Uncover; put the prawns, pork and cuttlefish over the noodle mixture. Cover and cook for a further 2 minutes. Remove the lid, stir-fry the noodle mixture evenly over a high heat for a moment.

4. Push the noodle mixture to one side of the wok. Add another 2 tablespoons lard to fry the garlic till light brown. Add the light soya sauce and a ladleful of stock. Stir in the noodle mixture and stir-fry to mix evenly.

5. Lastly, add the chives and stir. Remove to a plate, garnish with C and serve hot.

6. Repeat process with the other half of the ingredients.

Note:
Use lard to fry as it gives a better flavour and aroma than ordinary cooking oil. Frying should be done over a high heat throughout to prevent the noodles from becoming soggy and to keep the bean sprouts crunchy.

[6 servings]

170 *Nasi Lemak Kukus*

(Steamed coconut milk rice)

625 g (22 oz) No 1 Thai rice
625 g (22 oz) grated coconut, white
1½ teaspoons salt
285 ml (10 fl oz) water
  6 screw pine leaves, tied into a
     knot

1. Wash the rice several times until the water is completely clear. Leave it to soak overnight. Drain before use.
2. Use a piece of muslin to squeeze the coconut for 225 ml (8 fl oz) No 1 milk. Strain. Stir in the salt and set aside.
3. Add water to the grated coconut and squeeze again to obtain 225 ml (8 fl oz) No 2 milk.
4. Place the rice and screw pine leaves in a steamer. Use the handle end of a wooden spoon to make about five steam holes in the rice for the steam to circulate. Steam the rice over rapidly boiling water for 20 minutes.
5. Remove the steamed rice to a saucepan. Pour in the No 2 milk. Stir the rice well and keep it covered for 10 minutes. Return the rice to the steamer and re-steam for another 10 minutes.
6. Transfer the rice to the saucepan again to mix in the No 1 milk. Cover for 5 minutes then return it to the steamer to steam for another 5 minutes. Serve hot or cold.

Note:
Make steam holes in the rice each time you re-steam it. This allows a greater circulation of steam so that the rice will be soft without being soggy.

[8 servings]

171 *Nasi Kuning*

(Yellow rice)

625 g (22 oz) bryani rice
  2 tablespoons oil

A
  1 teaspoon pounded ginger
  4 cloves garlic
  6 shallots, thinly sliced

B
  8 cm (3 in) piece cinnamon bark
  8 cardamons, lightly bashed
  8 cloves

C
115 g (4 oz) ghee or butter
  ½ teaspoon turmeric powder blended with 1 tablespoon lime juice

995 ml (35 fl oz) boiling water

D
  1 teaspoon monosodium glutamate
  1 rounded teaspoon salt
  1 chicken cube

  55 g (2 oz) almonds, chopped
115 g (4 oz) sultanas

1. Wash the rice and drain it in a colander.
2. Heat an iron wok (kuali). Heat the oil and brown *A* in the given order.
3. Add *B* and stir-fry. Add *C*.
4. Add the rice and stir-fry till the oil is absorbed.
5. Remove the rice to a saucepan or an electric rice cooker. Pour in the

boiling water and season with *D*. Boil with the lid on over a moderate heat till the rice has absorbed all the water. Reduce the heat to low and cook for another 15 minutes. Spoon the cooked rice on to a large platter. Garnish with a sprinkling of fried almonds and sultanas.

To fry the almonds and sultanas:

1. Place 3 tablespoons oil in a heated pan to stir-fry the chopped almonds till light brown, over a low heat. Drain on absorbent paper. Store in a bottle.

2. In the same oil, fry the sultanas for 2 minutes. Drain and cool on absorbent paper.

[8 servings]

A {
170 g (6 oz) streaky pork
455 ml (16 fl oz) water
$\frac{1}{4}$ teaspoon salt
}

310 g (11 oz) small prawns
455 ml (16 fl oz) water
4 tablespoons lard or oil
1 tablespoon pounded garlic

B {
1 tablespoon preserved soya beans, pounded
$\frac{1}{2}$ teaspoon salt
1 teaspoon monosodium glutamate
$\frac{1}{2}$ teaspoon pepper
1 teaspoon sugar
}

C {
170 g (6 oz) water convolvulus cut into short lengths
625 g (22 oz) bean sprouts, washed and picked
625 g (22 oz) fresh yellow noodles
}

D {
1 cucumber, without skin and centre, shredded very finely into 4 cm lengths
2 eggs, fried into thin omelettes and finely shredded
3 tablespoons fried crispy shallots*
3 red chillies, slit, seeded and shredded as for cucumber
Dash of pepper
1 bundle coriander leaves
}

1. Boil the streaky pork in *A* for 20 minutes. Set aside the stock and cut the boiled pork into thin strips.

2. Shell the prawns. Wash and drain the shells in a colander. Pound the shells coarsely, adding the 455 ml water. Stir and strain liquid into a bowl.

3. Heat the lard in a heated iron wok (kuali) to fry the pounded garlic till light brown. Add and stir-fry *B* for a minute.

4. Pour in the prawn liquid, pork stock and bring to the boil. Add the prawns and the streaky pork to cook for a minute.

5. Add *C* to the boiled mixture. Stir-fry for 2–3 minutes over a high heat to cook the noodles.

6. Dish on to a large plate and garnish with *D*. Serve hot.

To garnish:
Arrange cucumber, eggs, crispy shallots, red chillies, pepper, and coriander leaves, attractively.

See "Helpful Hints".

[10 servings]

173 *Pork Congee*
豬肉粥

A {
225 g (½ lb) pork liver, thinly sliced
1 tablespoon ginger juice
1 teaspoon light soya sauce

B {
1 teaspoon light soya sauce
1 teaspoon monosodium glutamate
¼ teaspoon sesame oil
½ teaspoon salt
1 teaspoon cornflour
Dash of pepper

C {
340 g (¾ lb) minced pork, lean with a little fat
4 tablespoons preserved radish, chopped finely
225 g (8 oz) rice, washed and drained

D {
2 teaspoons salt
1 tablespoon lard or oil
2·5 litres (80 fl oz) water

E {
4 stalks spring onions, cut finely
5 pairs crispy Chinese crullers cut into pieces
Dash of pepper

1. Season liver with *A*.
2. Mix *B* in a bowl. Add *C* and mix well.
3. Mix *D* with the rice. Boil the water. Add the rice, cover the pan and bring it to the boil again. Reduce the heat and let it simmer until the congee is thick and smooth. Stir occasionally.
4. Shape the pork into small meat balls, and drop them into the boiling congee. Cook till the meat is well done. Add the liver but do not over-cook.
5. Dish the congee, with some of the meat balls and liver, into individual bowls. Garnish with *E* and serve hot.

Note:
If the congee is too thick, add water to obtain the consistency required before adding the pork and liver. To obtain a gluey consistency, add 1 tablespoon glutinous rice to cook with the rice.

[10 servings]

174 *Steamed Glutinous Rice*
糯米飯

A {
1 piece dried streaky pork*
6 dried Chinese mushrooms, soaked
2 pairs Chinese sausages

B {
1 teaspoon ginger
1 teaspoon garlic

C {
310 g (11 oz) pork bones
680 ml (24 fl oz) water
¼ teaspoon salt
1 teaspoon peppercorns
4 tablespoons lard
10 shallots, thinly sliced
625 g (22 oz) glutinous rice, washed, soaked overnight and drained

D {
2 teaspoons dark soya sauce
1 teaspoon monosodium glutamate
1 teaspoon sesame oil

1. Dice *A* and chop *B*.
2. Boil *C* and let it simmer gently until the stock is reduced to 400 ml (14 fl oz), approximately 1 hour. Strain.
3. Heat an iron wok (kuali). Heat the lard to brown the chopped ingredients and the shallots. Add the diced ingredients and stir-fry for a minute. Add the glutinous rice and mix it thoroughly with the fried mixture.

Pour in the stock. Season with *D* and stir-fry for a moment.

4. Reduce the heat to very low. Cover the wok and cook for a further 5 minutes till the stock is absorbed.

5. Remove the cooked glutinous rice and press it down firmly into small bowls. Place the bowls in a steamer and steam for 20 minutes. Serve hot.

This is the seasoned, dried variety imported from China.

Note:
For 'Glutinous rice with chicken', use fried chicken pieces seasoned with a little salt, monosodium glutamate and light soya sauce. Leave out the streaky pork. Cut the sausages and mushrooms into big pieces instead of small cubes. The method is similar.

Steamed Glutinous Rice

171

175 *Nasi Kunyit*

(Yellow glutinous rice)

625 g (22 oz) glutinous rice
　1 tablespoon pounded turmeric
　2 tablespoons lemon juice
　　Water
625 g (22 oz) grated coconut, white
　1½ teaspoons salt
　6 screw pine leaves, tied into a
　　knot

1. Wash the rice till clean. Rub in the pounded turmeric. Add the lemon juice. Add water to come up to 5 cm (2 in) above rice in a bowl and soak overnight. Squeeze the grated coconut for No 1 milk. Stir in the salt. Set aside. Add water to the grated coconut and squeeze again to obtain 170 ml (6 fl oz) No 2 milk.

2. Drain the rice in a colander. Place the rice and screw pine leaves in a steamer. Steam for 15 minutes over rapidly boiling water.

3. Remove the rice to a saucepan, stir in the No 2 milk and cover for 5 minutes. Bring the rice back to the steamer to re-steam for another 7 minutes.

4. Transfer the rice to the saucepan again and stir in the No 1 milk. Cover for 3 minutes. Re-steam for another 5 minutes.

Note:
The steamed rice can be pressed firmly in a tray and cut into pieces when cold.

Make steam holes as for Nasi Lemak Kukus (page 168).

Itek Tim (176)

SOUPS

176 Itek Tim

(Salted Chinese mustard duck soup)

565 g (20 oz) preserved salted
    Chinese mustard
1 duck, cut into four pieces
1 tablespoon brandy
3·6 litres (128 fl oz) water

A {
    4 dried tamarind slices
    2 thick slices ginger
    4 salted plums

B {
    625 g ($1\frac{3}{4}$ lb) pig's foreleg, cut
      into pieces
    $\frac{1}{2}$ tablespoon brandy
    2 teaspoons salt
    1 teaspoon monosodium
      glutamate

1. Cut the salted mustard into big pieces and soak in water for $\frac{1}{2}$ hour. Drain.
2. Season the duck with brandy.
3. Boil the water. Add the duck, salted mustard and A. When the water re-boils, add B.
4. Let the soup boil rapidly for 10 minutes. Lower the heat and let simmer till the meat is tender, about $1-1\frac{1}{2}$ hours.

Note:
You may add four tomatoes [quartered] during the last 10 minutes of the cooking time.

177 Chicken And Corn Soup

1·2 kg ($2\frac{1}{2}$ lb) chicken
4 tablespoons water

A {
    1·4 litres (48 fl oz) water
    1 teaspoon salt
    1 teaspoon peppercorns

B {
    2 eggs, beaten with 2 table-
      spoons water
    $\frac{1}{2}$ teaspoon salt
    1 teaspoon monosodium
      glutamate
    1 teaspoon light soya sauce
    1 big can of creamed corn

C {
    4 tablespoons cornflour
    1 tablespoon plain flour
115 ml (4 fl oz) water

1. Cut the chicken into large pieces.
2. Mince the chicken breasts. Mix with the 4 tablespoons water and set aside.
3. Boil A in a saucepan. Add the cut chicken pieces, and let the soup simmer for $1\frac{1}{2}$ hours. Boil until three-quarters of the soup is left. Strain into another saucepan.
4. Add 225 ml (8 fl oz) soup to the minced chicken. Mix well.
5. Bring the rest of the soup to the boil rapidly. Add B, stirring slowly till the egg mixture floats to the top. Add the corn and the minced chicken and bring to the boil. Reduce the heat, blend C in a bowl and stir it in gradually.
6. Remove from the heat. Serve the soup in a large serving bowl.

178 *Soto Ayam*

(Indonesian chicken soup)

1·2 kg (2½ lb) chicken, whole, including cleaned liver and gizzard
1 teaspoon salt
1 tablespoon oil

A {
8 shallots, chopped coarsely
2 cloves garlic, bashed
1 teaspoon peppercorns
½ thumb-sized piece fresh turmeric
4 candlenuts, lightly bashed
1 thumb-sized piece ginger, lightly bashed
3 stalks lemon grass, bruised

B {
2–3 teaspoons salt
2 teaspoons monosodium glutamate
3·5 litres (128 fl oz) water

C {
1–2 tablespoons "chili padi", pounded finely
4 tablespoons dark soya sauce
1 teaspoon sugar

4 hard-boiled eggs, shelled and diced
225 g (8 oz) boiled potatoes, diced
30 g (1 oz) bean vermicelli, soaked in hot water

D {
4 sprigs Chinese celery, cut into pieces
2 stalks spring onions, cut into pieces
½ cup crispy shallots*
8 local lemons, cut into wedges

1. Wash the chicken and rub in 1 teaspoon salt. Set aside.
2. Heat oil in a pan to fry A over a high heat for ½ minute. Set aside.
3. Boil B in a saucepan. Put in A, the chicken, liver, and gizzard.
4. Cover the pan and let simmer for ¾ hour. Remove the chicken, liver, and gizzard to a basin of cold water for 10 minutes to cool.
5. Bone the chicken. Dice and put the meat aside. Return the bones to the stock. Boil gently for 1½ hours. Strain the stock and leave to simmer till ready to serve.
6. Mix C together in a bowl.
7. Place a little of the diced ingredients and the bean vermicelli in individual soup bowls. Add boiling soup and garnish with D. Add chillied sauce with a squeeze of local lemon to taste. Serve hot.

Refer "Helpful Hints".

179 *Sop Kambing*

(Mutton soup)

A {
205 g (10 oz) shallots
55 g (2 oz) garlic
115 g (4 oz) ginger
$\frac{1}{2}$ piece nutmeg
}

B {
2 teaspoons pepper
1 teaspoon turmeric powder
1 teaspoon cumin powder
2 tablespoons coriander powder
}

2 pairs sheep's trotters, cut into short lengths

1·8 kg (4 lb) mutton ribs, cut into pieces

C {
3·6 litres (128 fl oz) water
10 cm (4 in) piece cinnamon bark
20 cardamon seeds, bashed
1 cluster star anise
2 tablespoons salt
1–2 teaspoons monosodium glutamate
$\frac{1}{2}$ teaspoon bicarbonate of soda
}

D {
6 tablespoons plain flour
2 tablespoons quick cooking oats, pounded finely
2·3 litres (80 fl oz) water
}

E {
$\frac{1}{2}$ cup crispy shallots
15 sprigs Chinese celery, cut into pieces
}

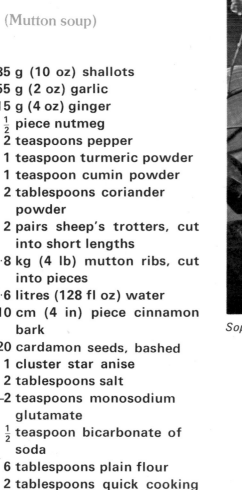

Sop Kambing

1. Pound *A* to a fine paste. Add *B* and mix thoroughly in a large bowl. Put in the meat to marinate for $\frac{1}{2}$ hour.
2. Boil *C*. Add the marinated meat and season with salt and monosodium glutamate. Boil rapidly for 20 minutes. Reduce the heat and let simmer for $1\frac{1}{2}$ – 2 hours or till the meat is tender.
3. Remove the trotters to a small saucepan, add 455 ml soup and the bicarbonate of soda. Let simmer till trotters are tender.
4. Pour the soup and trotters back into the saucepan of ribs. Mix and bring to the boil.
5. Blend *D* in a bowl and pour gradually into the soup. Stir till well-blended.
6. Let simmer until ready to serve. Serve hot.

To serve mutton soup:

Dish the soup and meat into a large bowl or serve in individual soup bowls. Garnish with *E*.

180 Stuffed Chicken Soup

40 g (1½ oz) bird's nest, cleaned
905 g (2 lb) small whole chicken, boned
2 slices ginger
2 teaspoons salt
½ teaspoon monosodium glutamate
1 slice cooked ham, shredded

1. Soak bird's nest in cold water overnight and drain in a sieve.
2. Stuff the bird's nest into the chicken through the opening at the neck. Tie a string below the opening.
3. Into a saucepan of rapidly boiling water, place the stuffed chicken, ginger slices, and 1 teaspoon salt. Cover the pan and cook for 5 minutes.
4. Remove the chicken and soak it in cold water for 5 minutes. Set aside. Boil the stock again; add the chicken bones and boil for ½ hour over a very high heat.
5. Strain stock with a piece of muslin and measure 1 litre (32 fl oz) for steaming the chicken. Add 1 teaspoon salt and ½ teaspoon monosodium glutamate to season. Place chicken and seasoned stock in a steamer. Steam gently for 2 hours. Serve hot in a deep bowl. Top with a sprinkling of shredded ham.

181 Tripe Soup

1 pig's tripe, cleaned
A {
1·8 litres (64 fl oz) water
1 teaspoon peppercorns
2 slices ginger
}
B {
625 g (1 lb 6 oz) pork bones, washed and cut into pieces
115 g (4 oz) gingko nuts
1 chicken cube
1 teaspoon salt
1 teaspoon monosodium glutamate
½ teaspoon sugar
2 teaspoons light soya sauce
}

1. Clean pig's tripe with salt and water. Turn it inside out. Sprinkle on 115 g (4 oz) sago flour and a handful of salt. Rub tripe on a rough surface to remove the slime. Scrape off the excess slime with a knife. Wash the tripe again in water and some vinegar. Drain.
2. Heat an iron wok (kuali) till very hot. Sizzle the tripe on both sides, without oil, for a minute. Remove and cook tripe in boiling water for another minute. Drain in a colander.
3. Boil A rapidly over a high heat.
4. Add B and the cooked tripe. Boil over a very high heat for 10 minutes.
5. Cover and let simmer for 1–1½ hours or till tripe is tender. Remove tripe and cut into small pieces to serve in the soup.

182 *Chicken And Macaroni Soup*

1 teaspoon salt

A {
1·2 kg (2½ lb) chicken, whole
3·7 litres (128 fl oz) water
1 tablespoon peppercorns
2 teaspoons salt
2 teaspoons monosodium glutamate
1 teaspoon sugar
}

B {
2 tablespoons light soya sauce
1 teaspoon monosodium glutamate
½ teaspoon sesame oil
}

225 g (8 oz) macaroni, boiled and drained

C {
4 tablespoons crispy shallots*
1 bunch coriander leaves
1 cup croutons
Dash of pepper
}

1. Rub 1 teaspoon salt over the chicken. Marinate for ½ hour.
2. Boil *A*.
3. Put in the chicken and bring to a rapid boil for 5 minutes. Cover the saucepan and let simmer for 40 minutes.
4. Remove and immerse the chicken in cold water for 10 minutes. Bone the chicken and return the bones to the soup. Let the soup simmer for 2 hours till it is reduced to 2·3 litres. Strain into another saucepan.
5. Shred or dice the chicken.
6. Mix *B* in a bowl. Add 4 tablespoons soup. Add the chicken and mix well.

To serve:

Place the macaroni in a large bowl and arrange the chicken on top. Add boiling soup and garnish with *C*.

See "Helpful Hints".

183 *Spicy Sparerib Consomme*

肉骨茶

625 g (1 lb 6 oz) pork sparerib, cut into small pieces

A {
½ teaspoon pepper
½ teaspoon salt
}

3 tablespoons lard
1 tablespoon sugar

B {
2 cloves garlic, bashed
1 teaspoon preserved brown soya beans, pounded
}

C {
2 segments star anise
2·5 cm (1 in) piece cinnamon bark
1 teaspoon peppercorns
1 teaspoon salt
1 teaspoon monosodium glutamate
1 teaspoon dark soya sauce
1·4 litres (48 fl oz) boiling water
1 tablespoon crispy shallots*
Crispy Chinese crullers, sliced
}

1. Marinate sparerib in *A* for ½ hour.
2. Heat pan till very hot. Add 2 tablespoons lard and fry sparerib till well-browned. Remove to a dish.
3. In a clean pan, heat 1 tablespoon lard and caramelize the sugar till light brown. Add *B*. Stir-fry for ½ minute,

then add the fried sparerib and *C*.

4. Let the consomme boil rapidly for 10 minutes, reduce the heat and let simmer for a further $1\frac{1}{2}-1\frac{3}{4}$ hours or till the meat is tender. Remove excess oil from the surface before serving.

5. Serve hot with cruller slices.

*See "Helpful Hints".

Spicy Sparerib Consomme

184 Pong Tauhu Soup

(Bean curd with meat ball soup)

625 g (1 lb 6 oz) prawns
1·4 litres (48 fl oz) water

4 small soya bean cakes
[approx. 340 g or 12 oz]
625 g (22 oz) young, boiled,
bamboo shoots

A {
310 g (11 oz) streaky pork
910 ml (32 fl oz) water
}

B {
1 tablespoon salt
1 teaspoon monosodium
glutamate
1 egg
1 teaspoon dark soya sauce
4 tablespoons oil
1 tablespoon fried crispy
garlic
1 teaspoon pepper
}

625 g (1 lb 6 oz) minced pork
2 tablespoons finely chopped
spring onions
2 tablespoons lard or oil
1 teaspoon pounded garlic

C {
1 tablespoon preserved
brown soya beans, pounded
1 teaspoon sugar
}

D {
1–1½ teaspoons salt
1 teaspoon monosodium
glutamate
}

1. Shell and devein prawns.
2. Wash, drain and fry the shells. Pound the fried shells and mix with 1·4 litres water. Strain and set aside.
3. Mince the prawns and soya bean cakes together till fine.
4. Cut the bamboo shoots into fine strips.
5. Boil A. Cut the pork into fine strips. Set aside the stock.
6. Mix B in a bowl. Add the minced ingredients and spring onions. Grease hands and roll mixture into walnut-sized balls. Place the meat balls on a tray.
7. Heat the lard and fry garlic till light brown. Add C. Stir-fry for a minute. Add the bamboo shoots and stir. Add the prawn and pork stock. Season soup with D. Boil for 15 minutes.
8. Add the meat balls and shredded pork to the boiling soup. Boil gently till the meat balls float to the surface. Keep boiling for 5 – 7 minutes. Remove from the heat.

Note:
Cut one of the meat balls to see that it is cooked right through.

185 Shark's Fin Soup

A {
905 g (2 lb) small chicken, cut
into four pieces
1·4 litres (48 fl oz) water
1 teaspoon peppercorns
}

B {
1 tablespoon oyster sauce
1 tablespoon light soya sauce
1 teaspoon monosodium
glutamate
1 teaspoon sherry or wine
Dash of pepper
}

C {
225 g (½ lb) steamed crab meat
115 g (¼ lb) prepared softened
shark's fins [already soaked
in alkaline water]
}

2 eggs, beaten with 2 tablespoons water

D {
5 tablespoons cornflour
55 ml (2 fl oz) water
}

2 tablespoons lard

1. Boil A. Let simmer till the stock is reduced to two-thirds, about 1–1½ hours. Strain into another saucepan. Return chicken stock to the boil.
2. Mix B in a bowl. Add to the stock with C. Bring to the boil. Add the beaten eggs, stirring gently till they rise to the surface.
3. Blend D and pour gradually into the soup, stirring all the time to prevent

curdling. Lastly, stir in the lard.
Serve hot.

Note:
You can buy softened shark's fins at certain supermarkets.

Top: Pong Tauhu Soup
Bottom: Shark's Fin Soup

A
- **310 g (11 oz) small cuttlefish**
- **310 g (11 oz) minced pork**
- **225 g ($\frac{1}{2}$ lb) prawns; shelled, deveined and chopped**
- **$\frac{1}{4}$ teaspoon salt**
- **$\frac{1}{2}$ teaspoon monosodium glutamate**
- **$\frac{1}{4}$ teaspoon cornflour**

680 ml (24 fl oz) water

B
- **1 teaspoon salt**
- **1 teaspoon monosodium glutamate**
- **1 chicken cube**

15 g ($\frac{1}{2}$ oz) bean vermicelli, soaked in hot water

C
- **2 sprigs Chinese celery**
- **2 cloves chopped garlic, fried in oil**
- **Dash of pepper**

1. Remove head, ink bag and backbone from each cuttlefish. Set aside the heads. Wash and clean the inside of the cuttlefish. Drain cuttlefish in a colander.

2. Mix *A* thoroughly to stuff three-quarters of each cuttlefish. Fix the head back. Shape little meat balls with the remaining meat.

3. Boil the water in a saucepan. Add the stuffed cuttlefish and meat balls. Boil for 3 minutes. Season with *B*. Cut up the bean vermicelli and add to the soup. Garnish with *C* and serve in a large bowl.

Note:
When cleaning the cuttlefish, remove the brown outer skin from the body. In this way, the soup remains clear. Before stuffing meat into the cuttlefish, make a slit at the tail end of the cuttlefish. This will prevent the heat from pushing the meat out.

VEGETABLES, CHILLI PASTE AND PICKLES

Penang Achar (187)

183

187 *Penang Achar*

(Mixed vegetable pickle — Penang-style)

kg ($8\frac{1}{4}$ lb) cucumbers
140 g (5 oz) salt
20 green chillies
20 red chillies
1 teaspoon lime paste

A {
310 g (11 oz) shallots
55 g (2 oz) turmeric
30 — 40 dried chillies *or* 6 — 8 tablespoons chilli paste
5 red chillies
570 ml (20 fl oz) oil
}

1 thumb-sized piece ginger,
thinly shredded

B {
570 ml (20 fl oz) rice vinegar
570 ml (20 fl oz) water
455 g (16 oz) sugar
4 tablespoons salt
}

C {
910 ml (32 fl oz) water
910 ml (32 fl oz) vinegar
2 tablespoons sugar
1 tablespoon salt
}

795 g (28 oz) cauliflower, cut
into flowerettes
2 carrots, peeled and cut
into strips
935 g (33 oz) cabbage, cut
into small pieces
455 g (16 oz) roasted peanuts,
pounded
8 tablespoons roasted

sesame seeds

1. Wash the cucumbers. Cut off the ends. Halve each cucumber length- wise. Cut each half into two or three pieces lengthwise. Remove the seeds and soft centres.
2. Place as many cucumber strips as you can on a chopping board and cut them into 5 cm (2 in) lengths. Make a slit half-way down each piece.
3. Place the cucumber strips in a basin, sprinkle the salt, mix well and leave to season for 4 — 5 hours. Rinse, drain and squeeze in handfuls, using a piece of muslin. Set aside.
4. Slit the centre of the chillies to re- move the seeds. Soak the chillies in a bowl of water with 1 teaspoon lime paste for 2 — 3 hours. Drain till dry in a colander. [Do not wash after soaking in lime water.] Stuff chillies [see instructions].
5. Pound A to a fine paste.
6. Heat an aluminium wok (kuali). Heat oil to fry the shredded ginger till light brown.
7. Add the paste (Step 5) and stir-fry till fragrant and oil comes up to the

surface.
8. Add B and bring to the boil. Boil for a minute and remove to a bowl to cool completely.
9. Boil C rapidly to blanch the cucumbers, cauliflower, carrots and cabbages separately. Spread out to cool on large trays.
10. Heat an iron wok till very hot. Stir-fry the vegetables separately for $\frac{1}{2}$ minute with a little oil from the vinegar mixture. Spread on trays to cool.

To mix the pickle:
Place the fried vegetables, paste, pounded nuts, and sesame seeds in a large mixing bowl. Mix well and add the stuffed chillies. Leave overnight. Store in dry, clean bottles.

To stuff chillies:

A {
5 candlenuts
10 shallots
1 teaspoon shrimp paste
}

225 ml (8 fl oz) oil
$\frac{1}{4}$ teaspoon salt
2 tablespoons sugar
225 g ($\frac{1}{2}$ lb) dried prawns,
pounded finely

188 *Rebong Masak Lemak*

(Bamboo shoots in spicy coconut gravy)

1 medium-sized green pa-paya, skinned, finely grated and dried in the sun [optional]

1. Pound A.
2. Pour oil into a heated frying pan. Stir-fry the pounded paste till fragrant.
3. Stir in the salt and sugar.
4. Add the dried prawns and papaya and stir till well mixed. Fry for 5 minutes over a low heat. Cool on a tray before stuffing the chillies.

Note:
1. *Bring the vinegar water back to a rapid boil each time to blanch the vegetables. Spread the vegetables to cool to keep them crunchy.*
2. *Lime paste here refers to the white chalky edible lime that is used by betel-nut chewers. It can be bought from any Indian grocer. The crispness of the chillies can only be obtained by soaking them in the 'lime' water.*

A {
- 1 teaspoon peppercorns
- 2 teaspoons roasted coriander seeds
- 14 slices galangal
- $\frac{1}{2}$ thumb-sized piece turmeric
- 5 candlenuts
- 14 shallots
- 1 clove garlic
- 2 red chillies
- 2 tablespoons shrimp paste

455 g (16 oz) grated coconut
910 ml (32 fl oz) water
115 ml (4 fl oz) oil
2 stalks lemon grass

B {
- $\frac{3}{4}$ tablespoon salt
- 1 teaspoon sugar
- $\frac{1}{2}$ teaspoon monosodium glutamate

C {
- 455 g (16 oz) boiled, tender, bamboo shoots; sliced thinly
- 905 g (2 lb) chicken, cut into pieces
- 340 g (12 oz) pork ribs, cut into pieces

1. Pound A together in the given order to a very fine paste.
2. Use a piece of muslin to squeeze coconut for No 1 milk. Set aside.
3. Add water to the grated coconut and squeeze again for No 2 milk. Set aside.
4. In a very hot aluminium wok (kuali), heat oil to stir-fry paste and bruised lemon grass over a moderate heat, till oil bubbles through and paste is fragrant.
5. Add B and half of the No 2 milk. When mixture boils, add C to cook for 10 minutes, stirring occasionally.
6. Add the remaining No 2 milk. Stir and cover. Cook over a low heat for 20 minutes or till chicken is tender.
7. Finally, add the No 1 milk. Stir for a minute, remove from the heat.

189 *Chop Suey*

(Mixed vegetables)

115 g (4 oz) pork fillet, sliced
115 g (4 oz) pork liver, sliced

A {
1 teaspoon light soya sauce
$\frac{1}{2}$ teaspoon monosodium glutamate
1 teaspoon ginger juice
Dash of pepper
}

6 red chillies, seeded

B {
85 g (3 oz) canned bamboo shoots
115 g (4 oz) snow peas or French beans
Lard
}

455 g (1 lb) prawns, shelled and deveined
1 onion, peeled and quartered

C {
1 teaspoon monosodium glutamate
$\frac{1}{2}$ teaspoon salt
$\frac{1}{2}$ teaspoon sugar
2 tablespoons light soya sauce
1 tablespoon oyster sauce
$\frac{1}{2}$ tablespoon dark soya sauce
$\frac{1}{2}$ tablespoon sesame oil
$\frac{1}{2}$ tablespoon sherry or wine
4 Chinese mushrooms, soaked in hot water and sliced
1 can button mushrooms
}

Chop Suey

D {
1 tablespoon cornflour
170 ml (6 fl oz) water
}

1. Marinate pork and liver in *A* for 10 minutes.
2. Cut the chillies into thick long strips.
3. Slice *B* thinly. [Do not slice snow peas.]
4. Heat a pan till very hot, use 2 tablespoons lard to fry the prawns for $\frac{1}{2}$ minute. Remove to a dish. In the same pan, fry the following separately over a very high heat: onions, chillies, French beans or snow peas, bamboo shoots. Remove to a dish.
5. Mix *C* in a bowl. Heat 2 tablespoons lard in a clean pan and fry the mush-

Add the fried ingredients. Toss mixture in pan for a while. Add *C*, stir for a minute. Blend *D* and add. Stir-fry so that all the ingredients are mixed thoroughly. Remove from the heat and serve in a hot serving dish.

190 *Sambal Blachan*

(Chillied shrimp paste)

12 red chillies
$\frac{1}{2}$ teaspoon sugar
A pinch of salt
2 tablespoons toasted shrimp paste
Limes, cut into halves

1. Dip chillies in water.
2. Wash mortar and pestle. Do not wipe dry.
3. Put the chillies, sugar and salt in the mortar. Place the shrimp paste on top. Pound together till well-blended. Chillies should be pounded coarsely.
4. Keep in a freezer for future use. Squeeze lime juice on to the chillied shrimp paste before serving.

Note:
For extra flavour, pound one lime leaf till very fine before pounding the ingredients.

Salad—Nonya-style

191 *Salad — Nonya-style*

2 cucumbers
$\frac{1}{2}$ pineapple
A {
1 lime leaf, optional
$\frac{1}{4}$ teaspoon salt

B {
2 or 3 red chillies
2 tablespoons toasted shrimp paste

C {
2 – 3 tablespoons vinegar
$\frac{1}{2}$ – 1 tablespoon sugar
1 teaspoon lime juice

4 tablespoons dried prawns, pounded

1. Cut off the ends of each cucumber. Wash and dice cucumbers into 1 cm cubes [with skin].
2. Remove pineapple skin and dice pineapple into 1 cm cubes.
3. Pound A till fine. Add B and pound together till fine. Remove to a dish.
4. Add C to the shrimp paste mixture and stir till well mixed.

To mix the salad:
1. Place the cucumber and pineapple cubes in a large bowl. Add the dried prawns and mix thoroughly by hand.
2. Add the shrimp paste mixture, stir thoroughly, and serve.

Note:
Prepare all the ingredients in advance and store in a refrigerator. Stir in the shrimp paste mixture just before serving.

187

192 *Kachang Panjang Masak Lemak*

(Fried long beans)

A {
- 455 g (16 oz) grated coconut
- 225 ml (8 fl oz) water
- 55 g (2 oz) garlic
- 85 g (3 oz) shallots

Oil

- 2 red chillies, sliced
- 4 tablespoons oil
- 2 stalks lemon grass, sliced into thin rounds
- 1 teaspoon shrimp paste dissolved in 2 tablespoons water

B {
- 455 g (16 oz) long beans, cut into 7 mm ($\frac{1}{4}$ in) lengths
- 1 tablespoon sugar
- 1 teaspoon salt
- 455 g (1 lb) small prawns

1. Squeeze the coconut for No 1 milk. Set aside in a bowl. Add water to grated coconut and squeeze again for No 2 milk. Set aside.
2. Slice A finely. Heat an aluminium wok (kuali). Add oil and fry A till pale brown. Remove to a plate. Fry the chillies for a moment and remove to a plate.
3. In a clean wok, heat the 4 tablespoons oil to fry the lemon grass and shrimp paste for a minute. Add B and stir-fry for 2 minutes. Pour in the No 2 milk, stir and cook for 5 – 7 minutes or till beans are tender [but not too soft].
4. Add the prawns, stir for a minute. Reduce the heat to low, add the No 1 milk, stir and allow to cook for 3 minutes. Keep stirring till the prawns are cooked.
5. Add the fried ingredients, stir and remove to a plate. Serve hot or cold.

193 *Kelapa Goreng*

(Crispy coconut granules)

A {
- 10 shallots
- 2 red chillies
- 225 g (8 oz) grated coconut, white
- 115 g (4 oz) dried prawns, pounded finely
- 3 heaped tablespoons sugar
- 2 tablespoons oil

1. Pound A to a paste.
2. Fry grated coconut in a heated un-greased iron wok (kuali) over a moderate heat till crisp and pale brown, stirring all the time. Remove and pound lightly with pestle and mortar. Set aside in a bowl.
3. Mix the dried prawns and sugar with the paste (Step 1).
4. Heat an iron wok, add the oil and fry the dried prawn mixture over a moderate heat till almost dry. Reduce the heat to low, and fry till the dried prawns are light brown and crisp. Add the fried grated coconut.
5. Cool and store in an airtight, dry, clean bottle.

194 *Sayor Loday*

(Mixed vegetables in spicy coconut gravy)

A {
115 g (4 oz) shallots
1 clove garlic
1½ tablespoons shrimp paste
½ thumb-sized piece turmeric
2 candlenuts
5 dried chillies *or* 1 tablespoon chilli paste
Water
}

625 g (22 oz) grated coconut

B {
625 g (22 oz) cabbage, cut into small pieces
625 g (22 oz) long beans, cut into short lengths
310 g (11 oz) Chinese turnip, cut into thick short strips
4 tablespoons dried prawns, pounded finely
}

C {
1 tablespoon salt
3 tablespoons sugar
1 teaspoon monosodium glutamate
}

6 soya bean cakes, cut into quarters and fried
310 g (11 oz) green egg-plants, cut into wedges and soaked in salt water. Drain before use.
Oil
2 cloves garlic, thinly sliced
8 shallots, thinly sliced

2 tablespoons chilli paste

1. Pound A to a fine paste.
2. Add 225 ml (8 fl oz) water to the grated coconut and squeeze for No 1 milk. Set aside.
3. Add another 2 litres (70 fl oz) water to the grated coconut and squeeze again for No 2 milk. Pour into a saucepan.
4. Add paste and B to the No 2 milk. Season with C and bring to the boil.
5. Boil gently for ½ hour, add the fried soya bean cakes and egg-plants and cook for another 5 – 7 minutes or till egg-plants are cooked. Remove from the heat.
6. Heat a frying pan, heat 6 tablespoons oil and fry the sliced garlic and shallots till light brown. Reduce the heat.
7. Add the 2 tablespoons chilli paste and stir-fry for ½ minute. Pour in the No 1 milk and keep stirring till it comes to a boil. Remove and pour immediately over the boiled vegetables. Stir for another 2 – 3 minutes to release the heat from the gravy.

195 *Sambal Kangkong*

(Spicy water convolvulus)

A {
10 shallots
2 candlenuts
2 red chillies
1 teaspoon shrimp paste
}

225 ml (8 fl oz) water
225 g (8 oz) grated coconut
6 tablespoons lard or oil

B {
225 g (½ lb) small prawns, shelled and deveined
½ teaspoon salt
2 teaspoons sugar
}

625 g (22 oz) water convolvulus, cut into 8 cm (3 in) lengths

1. Pound A to a fine paste.
2. Add water to the coconut and use a piece of muslin to squeeze for milk. Strain.
3. Heat an iron wok (kuali) till very hot. Heat the lard and fry the paste until fragrant.
4. Add B and half of the coconut milk. Cook for a minute.
5. Add the water convolvulus and the rest of the coconut milk. Stir-fry over a high heat until they are just cooked but still crisp, about ½ minute. Remove to a plate and serve.

196 Apple And Potato Salad

A {
4 apples, skinned, cored and rinsed in salt water
455 g (16 oz) cucumber, without centre
225 g (8 oz) tomatoes, diced and drained
115 g (4 oz) green peppers
225 g (8 oz) carrots, par-boiled
455 g (16 oz) potatoes, boiled
4 hard-boiled eggs

B {
285 g (10 oz) salad cream
$\frac{1}{2}$ teaspoon salt
2 tablespoons sugar
1 tablespoon vinegar with 1 teaspoon dry mustard
4 tablespoons corn oil
1 small can thick cream

1. Dice A.
2. Mix B in a bowl and whisk till well blended.

To serve salad:

1. Mix all the diced ingredients, except the eggs, with three-quarters of the prepared salad cream in a large bowl.
2. Place in a deep dish and chill for 2 hours in the refrigerator.
3. Arrange the eggs over the chilled salad and pour the rest of the salad cream on top just before serving.

197 Hot Chilli Sauce

625 g (22 oz) red chillies
55 g (2 oz) dried chillies
910 ml (32 fl oz) water
8 cloves garlic
1 thumb-sized piece ginger, skinned and sliced
5 tablespoons salt
455 g (16 oz) sugar
170 ml (6 fl oz) rice vinegar

1. Remove stems from chillies.
2. Boil the dried chillies in some water in a saucepan. Let boil for 2 minutes. Leave to soak for 5 minutes. Wash chillies till the water is clear. Drain in a colander.
3. Put half of the chillies in an electric blender. Pour in 285 ml (10 fl oz) of the water and turn the control to high to blend chillies till very fine. Remove and set aside. Repeat process with the other half of the chillies, adding the garlic and ginger.
4. Combine the liquidized chilli mixture and the remaining water in an enamel saucepan. Add the salt and bring to the boil over a moderate heat, stirring constantly for 10 minutes.
5. Stir in the sugar. Bring chilli sauce to the boil. Lower the heat and continue simmering for $1\frac{1}{2}$ hours, stirring occasionally.
6. Add the vinegar, stir and continue boiling for 5 minutes. Remove from the heat. Cool before storing in dry, clean bottles.

198 Dried Chilli Paste

225 g (8 oz) dried chillies

1. Remove stems from chillies.
2. Place chillies in a saucepan. Add cold water to fill up to three-quarters of saucepan and bring to the boil.
3. Boil for 5 minutes. Cover pan and leave chillies to soak for 10 minutes. Drain. Place chillies in a large basin, wash till water is clear. Drain in a colander.
4. Using an electric blender, blend half of the chillies with 225 ml (8 fl oz) water till very fine. Remove paste and repeat process with the other half of the chillies and water.
5. Store chilli paste in a plastic container. Keep in freezer until needed.

Note:
Keep chilli paste rotating whilst blending. Add spoonfuls of water if paste is not rotating.

[Makes approximately 32 tablespoonfuls of chilli paste.]

199 Mixed Vegetable Pickle

A {
2 cucumbers
2 white radishes, skinned
2 carrots, skinned
4 red chillies, seeded
2 tablespoons salt
8 tablespoons sugar
115 ml (4 fl oz) vinegar
225 ml (8 fl oz) water
1 tablespoon salt
}

1. Wash and cut the cucumbers into 5 cm (2 in) lengths. Remove the centres. Cut the cucumbers, radishes, carrots and chillies into thin strips.
2. Place the cut vegetables in a basin. Sprinkle 2 tablespoons salt and mix thoroughly. Leave to stand for one hour. Rinse the vegetables and dry on a piece of muslin.
3. Pour A into an enamel saucepan and bring to the boil. Add the chilli strips for a second and remove, using a perforated ladle. Allow vinegar mixture to cool and add all the vegetables. Store the pickle in a dry clean bottle for one day; and keep in refrigerator until needed.

200 Salt Fish Pickle

A {
10 shallots
4 slices ginger
55 g (2 oz) sultanas [light colour]
2 tablespoons coriander seeds
½ tablespoon fennel
1 tablespoon cumin seeds
4 tablespoons sesame seeds, washed and drained
15 dried chillies
}

310 g (11 oz) salt fish [Penang ikan kurau]
Oil

B {
1 tablespoon sugar
2 tablespoons vinegar
110 ml (6 fl oz) water
}

1. Grind A to a fine paste.
2. Cut salt fish into small strips, fry in hot oil till light brown and crisp. Remove to a dish.
3. In a clean pan, heat 4 tablespoons oil. Fry the paste over a moderate heat till fragrant and the oil comes through.
4. Add B, stirring till almost dry. Cool the fried paste and add the fried salt fish. Mix well and store in a dry, clean bottle.

[Fills one jam bottle]

SELECTED

MENUS

Chinese Dinner: Chicken Wings (128), Almond Chicken (127), Roast Pork Strips (104) and Barbecued Pork
Sparerib (103), Fried Poh Pia (70), Pork Ribs in Sweet and Sour Sauce (117), Butterfly
Prawns (147), Sliced Beef Steak (111), Fried Rice (168), Chop Suey (189), Crab Omelette
(138), Shark's Fin Soup (185), Almond Jelly (62).

*Rich Fruit Cake (28), Kueh Lapis Beras (6),
Speckok Kueh Lapis Batavia (5) and
Kueh Khoo Moh Ho (4) on tray;
Bubor Cha-cha (59) in bowl.*

*Sop Kambing (179),
Satay (83).*

193

Gado-gado (78),
Mee Siam (69)

Braised Hot Pot (72),
Kueh Ko Swee (11).

194

Tauhu Goreng (85),
Mee Rebus (71).

Fried Radish Cake (80),
Flavoured Chicken Rice (167).

Apple and Potato Salad (196),
Nasi Pilau (164).

Salad—'Nonya'-style (191), Fried Mah Mee (172)

Fried Rice Noodles (77),
Seven-minute Crispy Chicken (124).

Rice Noodles In Beef Soup (82),
Steamed Radish Cake (90).

Groundnut Creme (63),
Spring Chickens (128).

Nasi Kuning (171),
Penang Achar (187),
Beef Serondeng (98),
Beef Rendang (106).

'Nonya' Family Re-union Dinner
Plain rice,
Babi Pong Tay (116),
Hati Babi Bungkus (110),
Pong Tauhu Soup (184),
Satay Babi (115),
Itek Tim (176),
Sambal Blachan (190),
Ayam Sioh (133).

Nasi Lemak Lunch
Nasi Lemak (162),
Otak-otak Panggang (74),
Penang Achar (187),
Kachang Panjang Masak Lemak (192),
Sambal Kangkong (195),
Sayor Loday (194).

199

LIST OF SOME INGREDIENTS AND SPICES

ENGLISH	MALAY	CHINESE	ENGLISH	MALAY	CHINESE
Agar-agar	Agar-agar	石花菜	Curry leaf	Daun kari	咖哩葉
Alkaline water (clear)	Ayer abu (puteh)	白鹼水	Dried bean curd wrapper	Tauhu kering	大腐皮
Alkaline water (yellow)	Ayer abu (kuning)	黃鹼水	Dried tamarind slice	Kulit asam	羅望片
Anchovies	Ikan bilis	江魚仔	Fennel seed	Jintan hitam	茴香子
Aniseed	Jintan manis	大茴香	Fenugreek	Halba	茴香花
Basil leaf	Daun kemangi	羅勒菜	Five-spice powder	Serbok lima rempah	五香粉
Bird's eye chilli	Chili padi	指天椒	Fried spongy bean curd	Tauhu bakar	豆腐泡
Borax	Tingkal	硼砂	Galangal	Lengkuas	藍薑
Candlenut	Buah keras	馬加拉	Garlic	Bawang puteh	蒜
Cardamon	Buah pelaga	豆蔻	Ginger	Halia	薑
Cashew nut	Biji gajus	檟如果	Gingko nut	Peck kway	白果
Chinese celery	Seladeri	芹菜	Granulated sugar	Gula pasir	砂糖
Chinese mustard greens	Sawi	菜心	Green beans	Kachang hijau	綠豆
Chinese parsley	Pasli	芫荽菜	Green pea flour	Tepong hoen kueh	綠豆粉
Chinese turnip	Bengkuang	蕪菁	Glutinous rice	Pulot	糯米
Chives	Kuchai	韮菜	Lemon grass	Serai	香芋
Cinnamon bark	Kayu manis	桂皮	Lime leaf	Daun limau purot	檸檬葉
Cloud ear fungus	Chendawan kering	木耳	Lime paste	Kapor	石灰乳
Clove	Bunga chengkeh	丁香	Local lemon	Limau nipis	星檸檬
Coriander leaf	Daun ketumbar	香菜	Local lime	Limau kesturi	酸柑
Coriander seed	Ketumbar	香菜子	Mint leaf	Daun pudina	薄荷葉
Crispy Chinese cruller	Yu char kuay	油條	Monosodium glutamate	Serbok perasa	味精
Cumin seed	Jintan puteh	小茴香	Mustard seed	Biji sawi	芥辣子

ENGLISH	MALAY	CHINESE	ENGLISH	MALAY	CHINESE
Nutmeg	Buah pala	荳蔻	Soya bean cake	Tauhu keping	豆腐乾
Onion	Bawang besar	洋葱	Soya bean strip	Tauhu kering	腐竹
Palm sugar	Gula Melaka	椰糖	Soya sauce	Kichap	醬油
Peppercorn	Biji lada	胡椒子	Spanish mackerel	Ikan tenggiri	鯖魚
Phaeomaria	Bunga kantan	香花	Spring onion	Daun bawang	葱
Polygonum	Daun kesom	古蒿葉	Star anise	Bunga lawang	八角
Poppy seed	Biji kas-kas	罌粟子	Star fruit	Belimbing	羊肚
Prawn paste	Petis	蝦膏	Sweet red sauce	Kichap manis merah	海鮮醬
Preserved bean curd	Tauhu asin	腐乳	Sweet thick black sauce	Kichap pekat manis	甜醬
Preserved soya bean	Tauchu	豆醬	Tamarind	Asam	羅望子
Rice noodle	Kway teow	粿條	Transparent bean vermicelli	Tang hoon	粉絲
Rice vermicelli	Mee hoon	米粉			
Rock sugar	Gula batu	冰糖	Turmeric	Kunyit	黃薑
Saffron	Safron	黃薑色	Turmeric leaf	Daun kunyit	黃薑葉
Sago flour	Tepong sago	西米粉	Water chestnut	Sengkuang China	馬啼
Salted plum	Plam asin	鹹梅	Water convolvulus	Kangkong	旱菜
Salted radish	Lobak asin	菜脯	Wet rice flour	Tepong beras basah	濕米粉（占）
Screw pine leaf	Daun pandan	香葉	White bean curd (soft)	Tauhu	豆腐
Sesame seed	Bijian	胡麻子	White radish	Lobak puteh	蘿蔔
Shallot	Bawang merah kechil	葱頭	Wolf herring	Ikan parang	西刀魚
Shrimp paste	Blachan	馬來羹	Yeast	Ragi	酵母
Soya bean	Kachang soya	黃豆	Yellow noodle	Mee	麵

INDEX OF SPICES, AND VEGETABLES

1. Skinned, split, black beans
2. Cloves
3. Green and white cardamons
4. Dried chillies
5. Cloud ear fungus
6. Candlenuts
7. Nutmegs
8. Dried turmeric
9. Star anise
10. Fenugreek
11. Cashew nuts
12. Coriander
13. Aniseed
14. Cinnamon bark
15. Dried lily buds or golden needles
16. White peppercorns
17. Black peppercorns
18. Poppy seeds
19. Saffron
20. Mustard seeds

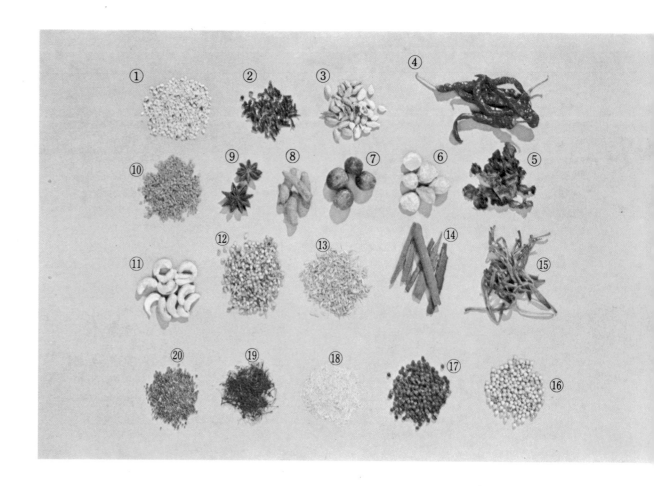

1. Water convolvulus
2. Lettuce
3. Local lettuce
4. Spring onions
5. Chives
6. Preserved salted Chinese mustard
7. Long beans
8. Curry leaves
9. Mint
10. Screw pine leaves
11. Parsley
12. Chinese parsley
13. Celery
14. Polygonum
15. Snow peas
16. French beans
17. Yam
18. Sweet potato
19. Ginger
20. Water chestnuts
21. White radish
22. Lemon grass
23. Bean sprouts
24. Young ginger
25. Star fruit
26. Turmeric leaf and turmeric
27. Chinese turnip
28. Sweet potato
29. Tapioca
30. Onions
31. Dried chillies
32. Local limes
33. Lime and lime leaves
34. Phaeomaria
35. Local lemons
36. Red chillies
37. Green chillies
38. Shallots

INDEX

The number in parenthesis refers to the recipe number. The second number refers to the page number.